Ninja Woodfire

Electric **BBQ Grill & Smoker**

Cookbook

2000 Days of Mouthwatering, Healthy Recipes to Improve Your Grilling Skills for Outdoor BBQ, Bake, Roast, Dehydrate, and More

HELEN J. BLANTON

Versatile cooking: grilling, **BBQ**, baking, dehydrating

Lots of mouth-watering and delicious recipes

From choosing ingredients to enjoying your meal, you're in control!

Improve your outdoor grilling skills

CONTENTS

Seafood 38

Meatless 47

INTRODUCTION

Greetings, I'm Helen J. Blanton, a dedicated culinary connoisseur with a lifelong love for the art of grilling and smoking. With a background in culinary arts and a deep-rooted passion for all things BBQ, I'm delighted to introduce you to the "Ninja Woodfire Electric BBQ Grill & Smoker Cookbook." This culinary masterpiece is the culmination of years of experience and a burning desire to share the secrets of successful grilling and smoking with you.

More than just a cookbook, it's your comprehensive guide to becoming a master of outdoor cooking. Amidst its pages, you'll find a wide array of meticulously crafted recipes tailored to the Ninja Woodfire Electric BBQ Grill & Smoker, promising flavor explosions with every dish. But this cookbook goes above and beyond; it's a kitchen companion designed to make your cooking experience a breeze. Inside, you'll encounter blank DIY recipe pages, inviting you to experiment and personalize your culinary creations. We've included organized shopping lists to simplify meal planning and ensure you have all the necessary ingredients at your fingertips. No more last-minute grocery runs or forgotten items.

To make your life easier, we provide precise cooking times, guaranteeing that each dish emerges perfectly cooked, every time. And if you're new to the world of grilling and smoking, fret not; our step-by-step instructions break down the process, demystifying it and making it accessible to all, regardless of your level of expertise.

My goal is to offer you a trusted resource that not only redefines outdoor cooking but also turns every meal into a flavorful adventure. The "Ninja Woodfire Electric BBQ Grill & Smoker Cookbook" is your passport to a world where taste, convenience, and the joy of culinary exploration converge. Join me on this flavorful journey, and together, we'll create unforgettable dining experiences that leave a lasting impression.

What is Ninja Woodfire Electric BBQ Grill & Smoker?

A Ninja Woodfire Electric BBQ Grill & Smoker is a versatile cooking appliance designed for outdoor grilling and smoking of various foods. This type of grill typically combines electric heating elements with the traditional flavor-enhancing aspect of wood or wood chips to provide the smoky flavor associated with barbecue cooking. It allows users to grill meats, vegetables, and other dishes at controlled temperatures while infusing them with the rich, smoky taste that is characteristic of traditional barbecue cooking methods. The electric element ensures precise temperature control, making it easier for users to achieve consistent results while eliminating the need for charcoal or open flames. This combination of electric convenience and wood-infused flavor makes the Woodfire Electric BBQ Grill & Smoker a popular choice for those who enjoy outdoor cooking.

How to cook the perfect BBQ?

1. SELECT QUALITY MEAT:

Start with high-quality cuts of meat such as ribs, brisket, pork shoulder, or chicken. The quality of your ingredients is crucial for great BBQ.

2. MARINATE OR SEASON:

Marinate the meat for several hours or overnight to infuse flavor, or use a dry rub to season it generously. Ensure the meat is at room temperature before cooking.

3. PREHEAT THE GRILL:

Preheat your BBQ grill to the appropriate temperature for the type of meat you're cooking. Use a thermometer to monitor the grill's temperature accurately.

4. CREATE INDIRECT HEAT:

For slow cooking, set up a two-zone fire by placing charcoal or wood on one side of the grill and leaving the other side without direct heat. This creates an area for indirect cooking.

5. ADD SMOKE FLAVOR:

If you want a smoky flavor, add soaked wood chips or chunks (such as hickory, mesquite, or applewood) to the coals or use a smoker box. Adjust the amount of smoke to your preference.

6. SEAR (OPTIONAL):

Start by searing the meat over direct heat for a few minutes on each side to develop a flavorful crust (optional for some cuts).

7. SLOW AND LOW COOKING:

Move the meat to the indirect heat side of the grill.

Maintain a consistent cooking temperature, typically between 225°F to 275°F (107°C to 135°C) for slow cooking. Use vents to control airflow and temperature.

8.BASTE OR MOP (OPTIONAL):

Periodically baste or mop the meat with a flavorful liquid (like BBQ sauce, marinade, or apple juice) to keep it moist and enhance flavor.

Cleaning of Ninja Woodfire Electric BBQ Grill & Smoker

After Each Use:

Turn Off and Unplug: Ensure the grill is turned off, and unplug it from the power source to ensure safety during cleaning.

Dispose of Ashes: If you used charcoal, allow the ashes to cool completely. Once cool, carefully remove and dispose of the ashes in a non-flammable container.

Empty Grease Tray: Remove the grease tray or pan and dispose of any accumulated grease and food particles. You can usually find this under the grill grates.

Clean the Grill Grates: Scrape off any remaining food residue from the grill grates using a grill brush or scraper. For stubborn grime, you can soak the grates in warm, soapy water and scrub them with a grill brush or sponge.

Periodic Cleaning:

Clean the Interior: Remove the cooking grates and any other removable parts to access the interior of the grill. Use a grill brush or scraper to re-move any built-up carbon deposits and ash from the grill's interior surfaces.

Wash Removable Parts: Wash removable parts such as grill grates, grease trays, and drip pans with warm, soapy water. Rinse thoroughly and allow them to dry before reassembling.

Check the Wood Chip Box: If your grill has a wood chip box or smoker box, empty and clean it to prevent the buildup of old wood chips and residue.

Clean the Exterior: Wipe down the exterior of the grill with a damp cloth or sponge. For stubborn stains, use a mild household cleaner or stainless steel cleaner if applicable. Be sure to follow the manufacturer's guidelines for cleaning the specific materials used in your grill's construction.

Inspect and Replace Parts: Periodically inspect the grill's components, including burners, heating elements, and gaskets. Replace any parts that are damaged or no longer functioning correctly.

Reassemble and Store: Once everything is clean and dry, reassemble the grill components and store the grill in a dry, protected area, or use a grill cover to protect it from the elements.

BREAKFASTST

BREAKFASTST

Supersized Family Pizza Omelet
Servings: 4 | Cooking Time: 10 Minutes

Ingredients:
- 10 large eggs
- 1 tablespoon Italian seasoning
- ½ cup pizza or marinara sauce
- 1 cup shredded mozzarella cheese
- 2 ounces pepperoni slices (about 24 slices)

Directions:
1. Insert the Cooking Pot and close the hood. Select GRILL, set the temperature to HI, and set the time to 10 minutes. Select START/STOP to begin preheating.
2. While the unit is preheating, in a medium bowl, whisk together the eggs and Italian seasoning.
3. When the unit beeps to signify it has preheated, pour the egg mixture into the Cooking Pot. Close the hood and cook for 5 minutes.
4. Place the Grill Grate next to the unit on top of the counter. After 5 minutes, open the hood and use a spatula to fold the egg sheet in half, then place it on top of the Grill Grate.
5. Place the Grill Grate into the unit. Top the omelet with the pizza sauce, mozzarella cheese, and pepperoni slices. Close the hood and cook for 5 minutes more.
6. When cooking is complete, the cheese will be melted. Remove the omelet from the grill and serve.

Grilled Breakfast Burritos
Servings: 4 | Cooking Time: 15 Minutes

Ingredients:
- 4 large eggs
- 12 slices bacon, cut into 1-inch pieces
- 1 cup frozen shredded hash browns
- 1 cup shredded Monterey Jack cheese
- 4 (10-inch) flour tortillas
- 2 tablespoons extra-virgin olive oil
- 4 tablespoons sour cream, for topping
- 1 avocado, pitted and diced, for topping

Directions:
1. Insert the Cooking Pot and close the hood. Select AIR CRISP, set the temperature to 390°F, and set the time to 15 minutes. Select START/STOP to begin preheating.
2. While the unit is preheating, in a medium bowl, whisk the eggs. Add the bacon, frozen hash browns, and cheese to the eggs and stir to combine.
3. When the unit beeps to signify it has preheated, pour the egg mixture into the Cooking Pot. Close the hood and cook for 10 minutes.
4. While the eggs are cooking, place the tortillas on top of the Grill Grate.
5. After 10 minutes, open the hood and use a silicone spatula to scramble the eggs and ensure the bacon is cooked. Remove the pot from the unit. Top the center of each tortilla with the scrambled egg mixture. Roll one end of the tortilla over the eggs, fold in the sides, and finish rolling the tortilla. Brush the olive oil over the burritos and place them seam-side down on the Grill Grate. Place the Grill Grate into the unit. Close the hood and cook for the remaining 5 minutes.
6. When cooking is complete, transfer the burritos to plates. Top with the sour cream and avocado and serve.

Egg And Sausage Stuffed Breakfast Pockets

Servings: 4 | Cooking Time: 23 Minutes

Ingredients:
- 1 package ground breakfast sausage, crumbled
- 3 large eggs, lightly beaten
- ⅓ cup diced red bell pepper
- ⅓ cup thinly sliced scallions (green part only)
- Sea salt, to taste
- Freshly ground black pepper, to taste
- 1 package pizza dough
- All-purpose flour, for dusting
- 1 cup shredded Cheddar cheese
- 2 tablespoons canola oil

Directions:
1. Select ROAST, set the temperature to 375°F, and set the time to 15 minutes. Select START/STOP to begin preheating.
2. When the unit beeps to signify it has preheated, place the sausage directly in the pot. Close the hood, and ROAST for 10 minutes, checking the sausage every 2 to 3 minutes, breaking apart larger pieces with a wooden spoon.
3. After 10 minutes, pour the eggs, bell pepper, and scallions into the pot. Stir to evenly incorporate with the sausage. Close the hood and let the eggs roast for the remaining 5 minutes, stirring occasionally. Transfer the sausage and egg mixture to a medium bowl to cool slightly. Season with salt and pepper.
4. Insert the Crisper Basket and close the hood. Select AIR CRISP, set the temperature to 350°F, and set the time to 8 minutes. Select START/STOP to begin preheating.
5. Meanwhile, divide the dough into four equal pieces. Lightly dust a clean work surface with flour. Roll each piece of dough into a 5-inch round of even thickness. Divide the sausage-egg mixture and cheese evenly among each round. Brush the outside edge of the dough with water. Fold the dough over the filling, forming a half circle. Pinch the edges of the dough together to seal in the filling. Brush both sides of each pocket with the oil.
6. When the unit beeps to signify it has preheated, place the breakfast pockets in the basket. Close the hood and AIR CRISP for 6 to 8 minutes, or until golden brown.

Mini Caprese Pizzas

Servings: 4 | Cooking Time: 10 Minutes

Ingredients:
- 1 (14-ounce) package refrigerated pizza dough
- 2 tablespoons extra-virgin olive oil
- 2 large tomatoes, thinly sliced
- 8 ounces fresh mozzarella cheese, cut into thin discs
- 12 fresh basil leaves
- Balsamic vinegar, for drizzling or dipping

Directions:
1. Insert the Grill Grate and close the hood. Select GRILL, set the temperature to MED, and set the time to 10 minutes. Select START/STOP to begin preheating.
2. While the unit is preheating, lay the pizza dough on a flat surface. Cut out 12 small round pizzas 1½ to 2 inches diameter each. Brush both sides of each dough round with the olive oil.
3. When the unit beeps to signify it has preheated, place the dough rounds on the Grill Grate, 4 across, in 3 rows. Close the hood and grill for 5 minutes.
4. After 5 minutes, open the hood and flip the rounds. Top each round with the tomato and cheese slices. Close the hood and cook for 5 minutes more.
5. When cooking is complete, remove the pizzas from the Grill Grate. Top each with the basil. When ready to serve, drizzle each pizza with the balsamic vinegar, or keep the vinegar on the side in a small bowl for dipping.

Sausage And Cheese Quiche

Servings: 4 | Cooking Time: 25 Minutes

Ingredients:
- 12 large eggs
- 1 cup heavy cream
- Salt and black pepper, to taste
- 12 ounces sugar-free breakfast sausage
- 2 cups shredded Cheddar cheese
- Cooking spray

Directions:
1. Select BAKE, set the temperature to 375ºF, and set the time to 25 minutes. Select START/STOP to begin preheating.
2. Coat a casserole dish with cooking spray.
3. Beat together the eggs, heavy cream, salt and pepper in a large bowl until creamy. Stir in the breakfast sausage and Cheddar cheese.
4. Pour the sausage mixture into the prepared casserole dish. Place the dish directly in the pot. Close the hood and BAKE for 25 minutes, or until the top of the quiche is golden brown and the eggs are set.
5. Remove from the grill and let sit for 5 to 10 minutes before serving.

Country-fried Steak And Eggs

Servings: 4 | Cooking Time: 16 Minutes

Ingredients:
- For the country-fried steak
- 1 cup milk
- 2 large eggs
- 2 cups all-purpose flour
- 2 teaspoons salt
- 1 teaspoon freshly ground black pepper
- 1 teaspoon garlic powder
- 1 teaspoon onion powder
- ¼ teaspoon cayenne pepper
- ¾ teaspoon paprika
- 4 (8-ounce) cube or round steaks
- For the eggs and gravy
- 4 to 8 large eggs
- 4 tablespoons (½ stick) unsalted butter
- 4 tablespoons all-purpose flour
- ½ cup heavy (whipping) cream
- ¼ teaspoon salt
- ¼ teaspoon freshly ground black pepper

Directions:
1. Create an assembly line with 3 shallow dishes. In the first dish, whisk together the milk and eggs. In the second dish, combine the flour, salt, black pepper, garlic powder, onion powder, cayenne pepper, and paprika. Place a steak in the flour mixture to coat both sides, then dip it into the egg mixture to coat both sides. Dip the steak back in the flour mixture, coating both sides. Place the coated steaks in the third shallow dish.
2. Insert the Grill Grate and close the hood. Select GRILL, set the temperature to HI, and set the time to 6 minutes. Select START/STOP to begin preheating.
3. When the unit beeps to signify it has preheated, place all 4 steaks on the Grill Grate. Close the hood and cook for 3 minutes.
4. After 3 minutes, open the hood and flip the steaks. Close the hood and cook for 3 minutes more.
5. When grilling is complete, transfer the steaks to a plate. Using grill mitts, remove the Grill Grate from the unit, leaving any excess fat drippings from the Grill Grate in the Cooking Pot.
6. Select AIR CRISP, set the temperature to 400°F, and set the time to 10 minutes. Select START/STOP and then press the PREHEAT button to skip preheating. Crack the eggs in the Cooking Pot. Close the hood and cook for 5 minutes, until the egg whites are opaque and firm. Remove the eggs from the pot.
7. Place the butter and flour in the Cooking Pot with the remaining fat drippings. Stir with a wooden spoon or silicone whisk until the butter has melted. Pour in the heavy cream and add the salt and pepper. Stir until completely mixed.
8. Close the hood and cook for 3 minutes. After 3 minutes, open the hood, stir the gravy, then close the hood to cook for 2 minutes more.
9. When cooking is complete, stir the gravy again and let it sit until you're ready to serve. To serve, pour the gravy over the country-fried steaks next to the eggs.

Coconut Brown Rice Porridge With Dates

Servings: 1 Or 2 | Cooking Time: 23 Minutes

Ingredients:
- ½ cup cooked brown rice
- 1 cup canned coconut milk
- ¼ cup unsweetened shredded coconut
- ¼ cup packed dark brown sugar
- 4 large Medjool dates, pitted and roughly chopped
- ½ teaspoon kosher salt
- ¼ teaspoon ground cardamom
- Heavy cream, for serving (optional)

Directions:
1. Select BAKE, set the temperature to 375ºF, and set the time to 23 minutes. Select START/STOP to begin preheating.
2. Place all the ingredients except the heavy cream in a baking pan and stir until blended.
3. Place the pan directly in the pot. Close the hood and BAKE for 23 minutes until the porridge is thick and creamy. Stir the porridge halfway through the cooking time.
4. Remove from the grill and ladle the porridge into bowls.
5. Serve hot with a drizzle of the cream, if desired.

Tomato-corn Frittata With Avocado Dressing

Servings: 2 Or 3 | Cooking Time: 20 Minutes

Ingredients:
- ½ cup cherry tomatoes, halved
- Kosher salt and freshly ground black pepper, to taste
- 6 large eggs, lightly beaten
- ½ cup corn kernels, thawed if frozen
- ¼ cup milk
- 1 tablespoon finely chopped fresh dill
- ½ cup shredded Monterey Jack cheese
- Avocado Dressing:
- 1 ripe avocado, pitted and peeled
- 2 tablespoons fresh lime juice
- ¼ cup olive oil
- 1 scallion, finely chopped
- 8 fresh basil leaves, finely chopped

Directions:
1. Put the tomato halves in a colander and lightly season with salt. Set aside for 10 minutes to drain well. Pour the tomatoes into a large bowl and fold in the eggs, corn, milk, and dill. Sprinkle with salt and pepper and stir until mixed.
2. Select BAKE, set the temperature to 300ºF, and set the time to 20 minutes. Select START/STOP to begin preheating.
3. Pour the egg mixture into a baking pan. Place the pan directly in the pot. Close the hood and BAKE for 15 minutes.
4. Scatter the cheese on top. Increase the grill temperature to 315ºF and continue to cook for another 5 minutes, or until the frittata is puffy and set.
5. Meanwhile, make the avocado dressing: Mash the avocado with the lime juice in a medium bowl until smooth. Mix in the olive oil, scallion, and basil and stir until well incorporated.
6. Let the frittata cool for 5 minutes and serve alongside the avocado dressing.

Grilled Kielbasa And Pineapple Kebabs

Servings: 4 | Cooking Time: 12 Minutes

Ingredients:
- ½ cup soy sauce
- ¼ cup light brown sugar, packed
- 2 (8-ounce) cans pineapple chunks, drained
- 2 (12-ounce) packages kielbasa sausages, cut into ½-inch slices

Directions:
1. In a large bowl, mix together the soy sauce, brown sugar, and pineapple chunks until the sugar is dissolved. Add the sausage slices and set aside for 10 minutes.
2. Thread the kielbasa and pineapple onto 10 to 12 skewers, alternating meat and fruit. Set aside any glaze that remains in the bowl.
3. Insert the Grill Grate and close the hood. Select GRILL, set the temperature to HI, and set the time to 12 minutes. Select START/STOP to begin preheating.
4. When the unit beeps to signify it has preheated, place half of the skewers on the Grill Grate. Brush them with extra glaze. Close the hood and grill for 3 minutes.
5. After 3 minutes, open the hood and flip the skewers. Close the hood and cook for 3 minutes more. After a total of 6 minutes, remove the skewers. Repeat with the remaining skewers.
6. When cooking is complete, remove the skewers from the grill and serve.

Egg And Bacon Nests

Servings:12 | Cooking Time: 30 Minutes

Ingredients:
- 3 tablespoons avocado oil
- 12 slices bacon
- 12 eggs
- Salt
- Freshly ground black pepper

Directions:
1. Insert the Grill Grate and close the hood. Select GRILL, set the temperature to HI, and set the time to 30 minutes. Select START/STOP to begin preheating.
2. While the unit is preheating, brush the avocado oil in the bottom and on the sides of two 6-cup muffin tins. Wrap a bacon slice around the inside of each muffin cup, then crack an egg into each cup. Season to taste with salt and pepper.
3. When the unit beeps to signify it has preheated, place one muffin tin in the center of the Grill Grate. Close the hood and grill for 15 minutes.
4. After 15 minutes, remove the muffin tin. Place the second muffin tin in the center of the Grill Grate, close the hood, and grill for 15 minutes.
5. Serve immediately or let cool and store in resealable bags in the refrigerator for up to 4 days.

Cheesy Hash Brown Casserole

Servings: 4 | Cooking Time: 30 Minutes

Ingredients:
- 3½ cups frozen hash browns, thawed
- 1 teaspoon salt
- 1 teaspoon freshly ground black pepper
- 3 tablespoons butter, melted
- 1 can cream of chicken soup
- ½ cup sour cream
- 1 cup minced onion
- ½ cup shredded sharp Cheddar cheese
- Cooking spray

Directions:
1. Put the hash browns in a large bowl and season with salt and black pepper. Add the melted butter, cream of chicken soup, and sour cream and stir until well incorporated. Mix in the minced onion and cheese and stir well.
2. Select BAKE, set the temperature to 325ºF, and set the time to 30 minutes. Select START/STOP to begin preheating.
3. Spray a baking pan with cooking spray.
4. Spread the hash brown mixture evenly into the baking pan.
5. Place the pan directly in the pot. Close the hood and BAKE for 30 minutes until browned.
6. Cool for 5 minutes before serving.

Banana Churros With Oatmeal

Servings: 2 | Cooking Time: 15 Minutes

Ingredients:
- For the Churros:
- 1 large yellow banana, peeled, cut in half lengthwise, then cut in half widthwise
- 2 tablespoons whole-wheat pastry flour
- ⅛ teaspoon sea salt
- 2 teaspoons oil (sunflower or melted coconut)
- 1 teaspoon water
- Cooking spray
- 1 tablespoon coconut sugar
- ½ teaspoon cinnamon
- For the Oatmeal:
- ¾ cup rolled oats
- 1½ cups water

Directions:
1. To make the churros
2. Put the 4 banana pieces in a medium-size bowl and add the flour and salt. Stir gently. Add the oil and water. Stir gently until evenly mixed. You may need to press some coating onto the banana pieces.
3. Spray the Crisper Basket with the oil spray. Put the banana pieces in the Crisper Basket and AIR CRISP for 5 minutes. Remove, gently turn over, and AIR CRISP for another 5 minutes or until browned.
4. In a medium bowl, add the coconut sugar and cinnamon and stir to combine. When the banana pieces are nicely browned, spray with the oil and place in the cinnamon-sugar bowl. Toss gently with a spatula to coat the banana pieces with the mixture.
5. To make the oatmeal
6. While the bananas are cooking, make the oatmeal. In a medium pot, bring the oats and water to a boil, then reduce to low heat. Simmer, stirring often, until all the water is absorbed, about 5 minutes. Put the oatmeal into two bowls.
7. Top the oatmeal with the coated banana pieces and serve immediately.

Mixed Berry Dutch Baby Pancake

Servings: 4 | Cooking Time: 12 To 16 Minutes

Ingredients:

- 1 tablespoon unsalted butter, at room temperature
- 1 egg
- 2 egg whites
- ½ cup 2% milk
- ½ cup whole-wheat pastry flour
- 1 teaspoon pure vanilla extract
- 1 cup sliced fresh strawberries
- ½ cup fresh raspberries
- ½ cup fresh blueberries

Directions:

1. Select BAKE, set the temperature to 330ºF, and set the time to 16 minutes. Select START/STOP to begin preheating.
2. Grease a baking pan with the butter.
3. Using a hand mixer, beat together the egg, egg whites, milk, pastry flour, and vanilla in a medium mixing bowl until well incorporated.
4. Pour the batter into the pan. Place the pan directly in the pot. Close the hood and BAKE for 12 to 16 minutes, or until the pancake puffs up in the center and the edges are golden brown.
5. Allow the pancake to cool for 5 minutes and serve topped with the berries.

Grilled Egg And Arugula Pizza

Servings: 2 | Cooking Time: 8 Minutes

Ingredients:

- 2 tablespoons all-purpose flour, plus more as needed
- ½ store-bought pizza dough
- 1 tablespoon canola oil, divided
- 1 cup fresh ricotta cheese
- 4 large eggs
- Sea salt, to taste
- Freshly ground black pepper, to taste
- 4 cups arugula, torn
- 1 tablespoon extra-virgin olive oil
- 1 teaspoon freshly squeezed lemon juice
- 2 tablespoons grated Parmesan cheese

Directions:

1. Insert the Grill Grate and close the hood. Select GRILL, set the temperature to MAX, and set the time to 7 minutes. Select START/STOP to begin preheating.
2. While the unit is preheating, dust a clean work surface with flour. Place the dough on the floured surface and roll it into a 9-inch round of even thickness. Dust your rolling pin and work surface with additional flour, as needed, to ensure the dough does not stick.
3. Brush the surface of the rolled-out dough evenly with ½ tablespoon of canola oil. Flip the dough over and brush with the remaining ½ tablespoon oil. Poke the dough with a fork 5 or 6 times across its surface to prevent air pockets from forming during cooking.
4. When the unit beeps to signify it has preheated, place the dough on the Grill Grate. Close the hood and GRILL for 4 minutes.
5. After 4 minutes, flip the dough, then spoon teaspoons of ricotta cheese across the surface of the dough, leaving a 1-inch border around the edges.
6. Crack one egg into a ramekin or small bowl. This way you can easily remove any shell that may break into the egg and keep the yolk intact. Imagine the dough is split into four quadrants. Pour one egg into each. Repeat with the remaining 3 eggs. Season the pizza with salt and pepper.
7. Close the hood and continue cooking for the remaining 3 to 4 minutes until the egg whites are firm.
8. Meanwhile, in a medium bowl, toss together the arugula, oil, and lemon juice, and season with salt and pepper.
9. Transfer the pizza to a cutting board and let it cool. Top it with the arugula mixture, drizzle with olive oil, if desired, and sprinkle with Parmesan cheese. Cut into pieces and serve.

Chicken Breakfast Sausages

Servings:8 | Cooking Time: 8 To 12 Minutes

Ingredients:
- 1 Granny Smith apple, peeled and finely chopped
- 2 tablespoons apple juice
- 2 garlic cloves, minced
- 1 egg white
- $\frac{1}{3}$ cup minced onion
- 3 tablespoons ground almonds
- $\frac{1}{8}$ teaspoon freshly ground black pepper
- 1 pound ground chicken breast

Directions:
1. Insert the Crisper Basket and close the hood. Select AIR CRISP, set the temperature to 330ºF, and set the time to 12 minutes. Select START/STOP to begin preheating.
2. Combine all the ingredients except the chicken in a medium mixing bowl and stir well.
3. Add the chicken breast to the apple mixture and mix with your hands until well incorporated.
4. Divide the mixture into 8 equal portions and shape into patties. Arrange the patties in the Crisper Basket. You may need to work in batches depending on the size of your Crisper Basket.
5. Close the hood and AIR CRISP for 8 to 12 minutes, or until a meat thermometer inserted in the center of the chicken reaches at least 165ºF.
6. Remove from the grill to a plate and repeat with the remaining patties.
7. Let the chicken cool for 5 minutes and serve warm.

Fried Potatoes With Peppers And Onions

Servings: 4 | Cooking Time: 35 Minutes

Ingredients:
- 1 pound red potatoes, cut into ½-inch dices
- 1 large red bell pepper, cut into ½-inch dices
- 1 large green bell pepper, cut into ½-inch dices
- 1 medium onion, cut into ½-inch dices
- 1½ tablespoons extra-virgin olive oil
- 1¼ teaspoons kosher salt
- ¾ teaspoon sweet paprika
- ¾ teaspoon garlic powder
- Freshly ground black pepper, to taste

Directions:
1. Insert the Crisper Basket and close the hood. Select AIR CRISP, set the temperature to 350ºF, and set the time to 35 minutes. Select START/STOP to begin preheating.
2. Mix together the potatoes, bell peppers, onion, oil, salt, paprika, garlic powder, and black pepper in a large mixing and toss to coat.
3. Transfer the potato mixture to the Crisper Basket. Close the hood and AIR CRISP for 35 minutes, or until the potatoes are nicely browned. Shake the basket three times during cooking.
4. Remove from the basket to a plate and serve warm.

Apple And Walnut Muffins

Servings:8 | Cooking Time: 10 Minutes

Ingredients:
- 1 cup flour
- 1/3 cup sugar
- 1 teaspoon baking powder
- ¼ teaspoon baking soda
- ¼ teaspoon salt
- 1 teaspoon cinnamon
- ¼ teaspoon ginger
- ¼ teaspoon nutmeg
- 1 egg
- 2 tablespoons pancake syrup, plus 2 teaspoons
- 2 tablespoons melted butter, plus 2 teaspoons
- ¾ cup unsweetened applesauce
- ½ teaspoon vanilla extract
- ¼ cup chopped walnuts
- ¼ cup diced apple

Directions:
1. Select BAKE, set the temperature to 330ºF, and set the time to 10 minutes. Select START/STOP to begin preheating.
2. In a large bowl, stir together the flour, sugar, baking powder, baking soda, salt, cinnamon, ginger, and nutmeg.
3. In a small bowl, beat egg until frothy. Add syrup, butter, applesauce, and vanilla and mix well.
4. Pour egg mixture into dry ingredients and stir just until moistened.
5. Gently stir in nuts and diced apple.
6. Divide batter among 8 parchment paper-lined muffin cups.
7. Put 4 muffin cups in the pot. Close the hood and BAKE for 10 minutes.
8. Repeat with remaining 4 muffins or until toothpick inserted in center comes out clean.
9. Serve warm.

Avocado Quesadillas

Servings: 4 | Cooking Time: 11 Minutes

Ingredients:
- 4 eggs
- 2 tablespoons skim milk
- Salt and ground black pepper, to taste
- Cooking spray
- 4 flour tortillas
- 4 tablespoons salsa
- 2 ounces Cheddar cheese, grated
- ½ small avocado, peeled and thinly sliced

Directions:
1. Select BAKE, set the temperature to 270ºF, and set the time to 8 minutes. Select START/STOP to begin preheating.
2. Beat together the eggs, milk, salt, and pepper.
3. Spray a baking pan lightly with cooking spray and add egg mixture.
4. Place the pan directly in the pot. Close the hood and BAKE for 8 minutes, stirring every 1 to 2 minutes, until eggs are scrambled to the liking. Remove and set aside.
5. Spray one side of each tortilla with cooking spray. Flip over.
6. Divide eggs, salsa, cheese, and avocado among the tortillas, covering only half of each tortilla.
7. Fold each tortilla in half and press down lightly. Increase the temperature of the grill to 390ºF.
8. Put 2 tortillas in Crisper Basket and AIR CRISP for 3 minutes or until cheese melts and outside feels slightly crispy. Repeat with remaining two tortillas.
9. Cut each cooked tortilla into halves. Serve warm.

Veggie Frittata

Servings: 4 | Cooking Time: 8 To 12 Minutes

Ingredients:
- ½ cup chopped red bell pepper
- ⅓ cup grated carrot
- ⅓ cup minced onion
- 1 teaspoon olive oil
- 1 egg
- 6 egg whites
- ⅓ cup 2% milk
- 1 tablespoon shredded Parmesan cheese

Directions:
1. Select BAKE, set the temperature to 350ºF, and set the time to 12 minutes. Select START/STOP to begin preheating.
2. Mix together the red bell pepper, carrot, onion, and olive oil in a baking pan and stir to combine.
3. Place the pan directly in the pot. Close the hood and BAKE for 4 to 6 minutes, or until the veggies are soft. Stir once during cooking.
4. Meantime, whisk together the egg, egg whites, and milk in a medium bowl until creamy.
5. When the veggies are done, pour the egg mixture over the top. Scatter with the Parmesan cheese.
6. Bake for an additional 4 to 6 minutes, or until the eggs are set and the top is golden around the edges.
7. Allow the frittata to cool for 5 minutes before slicing and serving.

Posh Orange Rolls

Servings:8 | Cooking Time: 8 Minutes

Ingredients:
- 3 ounces low-fat cream cheese
- 1 tablespoon low-fat sour cream or plain yogurt
- 2 teaspoons sugar
- ¼ teaspoon pure vanilla extract
- ¼ teaspoon orange extract
- 1 can organic crescent roll dough
- ¼ cup chopped walnuts
- ¼ cup dried cranberries
- ¼ cup shredded, sweetened coconut
- Butter-flavored cooking spray
- Orange Glaze:
- ½ cup powdered sugar
- 1 tablespoon orange juice
- ¼ teaspoon orange extract
- Dash of salt

Directions:
1. Cut a circular piece of parchment paper slightly smaller than the bottom of the Crisper Basket. Set aside.
2. In a small bowl, combine the cream cheese, sour cream or yogurt, sugar, and vanilla and orange extracts. Stir until smooth.
3. Insert the Crisper Basket and close the hood. Select AIR CRISP, set the temperature to 300ºF, and set the time to 8 minutes. Select START/STOP to begin preheating.
4. Separate crescent roll dough into 8 triangles and divide cream cheese mixture among them. Starting at wide end, spread cheese mixture to within 1 inch of point.
5. Sprinkle nuts and cranberries evenly over cheese mixture.
6. Starting at wide end, roll up triangles, then sprinkle with coconut, pressing in lightly to make it stick. Spray tops of rolls with butter-flavored cooking spray.
7. Put parchment paper in Crisper Basket, and place 4 rolls on top, spaced evenly.
8. Close the hood and AIR CRISP for 8 minutes, until rolls are golden brown and cooked through.
9. Repeat steps 7 and 8 to AIR CRISP remaining 4 rolls. You should be able to use the same piece of parchment paper twice.
10. In a small bowl, stir together ingredients for glaze and drizzle over warm rolls. Serve warm.

Fluffy Pancake Sheet

Servings: 4 | Cooking Time: 12 Minutes

Ingredients:
- 3 cups pancake mix
- 1½ cups milk
- 2 eggs
- Nonstick cooking spray
- Unsalted butter, for topping
- Maple syrup, for topping

Directions:
1. Insert the Cooking Pot and close the hood. Select BAKE, set the temperature to 350°F, and set the time to 12 minutes. Select START/STOP to begin preheating.
2. While the unit is preheating, in a large bowl, whisk together the pancake mix, milk, and eggs.
3. When the unit beeps to signify it has preheated, spray the Cooking Pot with cooking spray. Pour the batter into the pot. Close the hood and cook for 12 minutes.
4. When cooking is complete, cut the pancake into squares. Top with the butter and maple syrup and serve.

Western Omelet

Servings: 2 | Cooking Time: 18 To 21 Minutes

Ingredients:
- ¼ cup chopped bell pepper, green or red
- ¼ cup chopped onion
- ¼ cup diced ham
- 1 teaspoon butter
- 4 large eggs
- 2 tablespoons milk
- ⅛ teaspoon salt
- ¾ cup shredded sharp Cheddar cheese

Directions:
1. Select AIR CRISP, set the temperature to 390°F, and set the time to 6 minutes. Select START/STOP to begin preheating.
2. Put the bell pepper, onion, ham, and butter in a baking pan and mix well. Place the pan directly in the pot.
3. Close the hood and AIR CRISP for 1 minute. Stir and continue to cook for an additional 4 to 5 minutes until the veggies are softened.
4. Meanwhile, whisk together the eggs, milk, and salt in a bowl.
5. Pour the egg mixture over the veggie mixture.
6. Reduce the grill temperature to 360°F and BAKE for 13 to 15 minutes more, or until the top is lightly golden browned and the eggs are set.
7. Scatter the omelet with the shredded cheese. Bake for another 1 minute until the cheese has melted.
8. Let the omelet cool for 5 minutes before serving.

Pb&j

Servings: 4 | Cooking Time: 6 Minutes

Ingredients:
- ½ cup cornflakes, crushed
- ¼ cup shredded coconut
- 8 slices oat nut bread or any whole-grain, oversize bread
- 6 tablespoons peanut butter
- 2 medium bananas, cut into ½-inch-thick slices
- 6 tablespoons pineapple preserves
- 1 egg, beaten
- Cooking spray

Directions:
1. Insert the Crisper Basket and close the hood. Select AIR CRISP, set the temperature to 360°F, and set the time to 6 minutes. Select START/STOP to begin preheating.
2. In a shallow dish, mix the cornflake crumbs and coconut.
3. For each sandwich, spread one bread slice with 1½ tablespoons of peanut butter. Top with banana slices. Spread another bread slice with 1½ tablespoons of preserves. Combine to make a sandwich.
4. Using a pastry brush, brush top of sandwich lightly with beaten egg. Sprinkle with about 1½ tablespoons of crumb coating, pressing it in to make it stick. Spray with cooking spray.
5. Turn sandwich over and repeat to coat and spray the other side. Place the sandwiches in the Crisper Basket.
6. Close the hood and AIR CRISP for 6 minutes or until coating is golden brown and crispy.
7. Cut the cooked sandwiches in half and serve warm.

Cheesy Breakfast Casserole

Servings: 4 | Cooking Time: 14 Minutes

Ingredients:
- 6 slices bacon
- 6 eggs
- Salt and pepper, to taste
- Cooking spray
- ½ cup chopped green bell pepper
- ½ cup chopped onion
- ¾ cup shredded Cheddar cheese

Directions:
1. Place the bacon in a skillet over medium-high heat and cook each side for about 4 minutes until evenly crisp. Remove from the heat to a paper towel-lined plate to drain. Crumble it into small pieces and set aside.
2. Whisk the eggs with the salt and pepper in a medium bowl.
3. Select BAKE, set the temperature to 400°F, and set the time to 8 minutes. Select START/STOP to begin pre-heating.
4. Spritz a baking pan with cooking spray.
5. Place the whisked eggs, crumbled bacon, green bell pepper, and onion in the prepared pan. Place the pan directly in the pot. Close the hood and BAKE for 6 minutes.
6. Scatter the Cheddar cheese all over and bake for 2 minutes more.
7. Allow to sit for 5 minutes and serve on plates.

Mushroom And Squash Toast

Servings: 4 | Cooking Time: 10 Minutes

Ingredients:
- 1 tablespoon olive oil
- 1 red bell pepper, cut into strips
- 2 green onions, sliced
- 1 cup sliced button or cremini mushrooms
- 1 small yellow squash, sliced
- 2 tablespoons softened butter
- 4 slices bread
- ½ cup soft goat cheese

Directions:
1. Brush the Crisper Basket with the olive oil.
2. Insert the Crisper Basket and close the hood. Select AIR CRISP, set the temperature to 350ºF, and set the time to 7 minutes. Select START/STOP to begin preheating.
3. Put the red pepper, green onions, mushrooms, and squash inside the basket and give them a stir. Close the hood and AIR CRISP for 7 minutes or the vegetables are tender, shaking the basket once throughout the cooking time.
4. Remove the vegetables and set them aside.
5. Spread the butter on the slices of bread and transfer to the basket, butter-side up. Close the hood and AIR CRISP for 3 minutes.
6. Remove the toast from the grill and top with goat cheese and vegetables. Serve warm.

Sourdough Croutons

Servings:4 | Cooking Time: 6 Minutes

Ingredients:
- 4 cups cubed sourdough bread, 1-inch cubes
- 1 tablespoon olive oil
- 1 teaspoon fresh thyme leaves
- ¼ teaspoon salt
- Freshly ground black pepper, to taste

Directions:
1. Combine all ingredients in a bowl.
2. Insert the Crisper Basket and close the hood. Select AIR CRISP, set the temperature to 400ºF, and set the time to 6 minutes. Select START/STOP to begin preheating.
3. Toss the bread cubes and transfer to the basket. Close the hood and AIR CRISP for 6 minutes, shaking the basket once or twice while they cook.
4. Serve warm.

Banana Chips With Peanut Butter

Servings: 1 | Cooking Time: 8 Hours

Ingredients:
- 2 bananas, sliced into ¼-inch rounds
- 2 tablespoons creamy peanut butter

Directions:
1. In a medium bowl, toss the banana slices with the peanut butter, until well coated. If the peanut butter is too thick and not mixing well, add 1 to 2 tablespoons of water.
2. Place the banana slices flat on the Crisper Basket. Arrange them in a single layer, without any slices touching each another.
3. Place the basket in the pot and close the hood.
4. Select DEHYDRATE, set the temperature to 135ºF, and set the time to 8 hours. Select START/STOP.
5. When cooking is complete, remove the basket from the pot. Transfer the banana chips to an airtight container and store at room temperature.

Spinach With Scrambled Eggs

Servings: 2 | Cooking Time: 10 Minutes

Ingredients:
- 2 tablespoons olive oil
- 4 eggs, whisked
- 5 ounces fresh spinach, chopped
- 1 medium tomato, chopped
- 1 teaspoon fresh lemon juice
- ½ teaspoon coarse salt
- ½ teaspoon ground black pepper
- ½ cup of fresh basil, roughly chopped

Directions:
1. Grease a baking pan with the oil, tilting it to spread the oil around.
2. Select BAKE, set the temperature to 280ºF, and set the time to 10 minutes. Select START/STOP to begin preheating.
3. In the pan, mix the remaining ingredients, apart from the basil leaves, whisking well until everything is completely combined.
4. Place the pan directly in the pot. Close the hood and BAKE for 10 minutes.
5. Top with fresh basil leaves before serving.

Crustless Broccoli Quiche

Servings: 4 | Cooking Time: 10 Minutes

Ingredients:
- 1 cup broccoli florets
- ¾ cup chopped roasted red peppers
- 1¼ cups grated Fontina cheese
- 6 eggs
- ¾ cup heavy cream
- ½ teaspoon salt
- Freshly ground black pepper, to taste
- Cooking spray

Directions:
1. Select AIR CRISP, set the temperature to 325ºF, and set the time to 10 minutes. Select START/STOP to begin preheating.
2. Spritz a baking pan with cooking spray
3. Add the broccoli florets and roasted red peppers to the pan and scatter the grated Fontina cheese on top.
4. In a bowl, beat together the eggs and heavy cream. Sprinkle with salt and pepper. Pour the egg mixture over the top of the cheese. Wrap the pan in foil.
5. Place the pan directly in the pot. Close the hood and AIR CRISP for 8 minutes. Remove the foil and continue to cook another 2 minutes until the quiche is golden brown.
6. Rest for 5 minutes before cutting into wedges and serve warm.

Cinnamon Toast With Strawberries

Ingredients:
- 1 can full-fat coconut milk, refrigerated overnight
- ½ tablespoon powdered sugar
- 1½ teaspoons vanilla extract, divided
- 1 cup halved strawberries
- 1 tablespoon maple syrup, plus more for garnish
- 1 tablespoon brown sugar, divided
- ¾ cup lite coconut milk
- 2 large eggs
- ½ teaspoon ground cinnamon
- 2 tablespoons unsalted butter, at room temperature
- 4 slices challah bread

Directions:
1. Turn the chilled can of full-fat coconut milk upside down (do not shake the can), open the bottom, and pour out the liquid coconut water. Scoop the remaining solid coconut cream into a medium bowl. Using an electric hand mixer, whip the cream for 3 to 5 minutes, until soft peaks form.
2. Add the powdered sugar and ½ teaspoon of the vanilla to the coconut cream, and whip it again until creamy. Place the bowl in the refrigerator.
3. Insert the Grill Grate and close the hood. Select GRILL, set the temperature to MAX, and set the time to 15 minutes. Select START/STOP to begin preheating.
4. While the unit is preheating, combine the strawberries with the maple syrup and toss to coat evenly. Sprinkle evenly with ½ tablespoon of the brown sugar.
5. In a large shallow bowl, whisk together the lite coconut milk, eggs, the remaining 1 teaspoon of vanilla, and cinnamon.
6. When the unit beeps to signify it has preheated, place the strawberries on the Grill Grate. Gently press the fruit down to maximize grill marks. Close the hood and GRILL for 4 minutes without flipping.
7. Meanwhile, butter each slice of bread on both sides. Place one slice in the egg mixture and let it soak for 1 minute. Flip the slice over and soak it for another minute. Repeat with the remaining bread slices. Sprinkle each side of the toast with the remaining ½ tablespoon of brown sugar.
8. After 4 minutes, remove the strawberries from the grill and set aside. Decrease the temperature to HIGH. Place the bread on the Grill Grate; close the hood and GRILL for 4 to 6 minutes until golden and caramelized. Check often to ensure desired doneness.
9. Place the toast on a plate and top with the strawberries and whipped coconut cream. Drizzle with maple syrup, if desired.

SIDES, SNACKS & APPETIZERS

SIDES, SNACKS & APPETIZERS

Sweet Potato Fries With Honey-butter Sauce

Servings: 4 | Cooking Time: 20 Minutes

Ingredients:
- For the sweet potato fries
- 2 medium sweet potatoes, cut into ¼-inch-thick slices
- 3 teaspoons avocado oil
- 1 teaspoon salt
- ½ teaspoon paprika
- ½ teaspoon garlic powder
- ¼ teaspoon freshly ground black pepper
- For the honey butter
- 1 tablespoon honey
- 1 teaspoon powdered sugar
- 8 tablespoons (1 stick) salted butter, at room temperature

Directions:
1. Insert the Crisper Basket and close the hood. Select AIR CRISP, set the temperature to 400°F, and set the time to 20 minutes. Select START/STOP to begin preheating.
2. In a large bowl, drizzle the sweet potatoes with the avocado oil and toss to coat. In a small bowl, mix together the salt, paprika, garlic powder, and pepper. Sprinkle the seasoning over the sweet potatoes and toss gently to coat.
3. When the unit beeps to signify it has preheated, place the sweet potato fries in the Crisper Basket. Close the hood and cook for 10 minutes.
4. After 10 minutes, open the hood and shake the basket. Close the hood and cook for 5 minutes more. Open the hood again and shake the basket. If the fries are to your desired crispness, then remove them. If not, close the hood and cook up to 5 minutes more.
5. In a small bowl, whisk together the honey and powdered sugar until the sugar is dissolved. Add the butter and continue whisking. Serve alongside the fries.

Breaded Green Olives

Servings: 4 | Cooking Time: 8 Minutes

Ingredients:
- 1 jar pitted green olives
- ½ cup all-purpose flour
- Salt and pepper, to taste
- ½ cup bread crumbs
- 1 egg
- Cooking spray

Directions:
1. Insert the Crisper Basket and close the hood. Select AIR CRISP, set the temperature to 400ºF, and set the time to 8 minutes. Select START/STOP to begin preheating.
2. Remove the olives from the jar and dry thoroughly with paper towels.
3. In a small bowl, combine the flour with salt and pepper to taste. Place the bread crumbs in another small bowl. In a third small bowl, beat the egg.
4. Spritz the Crisper Basket with cooking spray.
5. Dip the olives in the flour, then the egg, and then the bread crumbs.
6. Place the breaded olives in the basket. It is okay to stack them. Spray the olives with cooking spray. Close the hood and AIR CRISP for 6 minutes. Flip the olives and AIR CRISP for an additional 2 minutes, or until brown and crisp.
7. Cool before serving.

Cheesy Summer Squash With Red Onion

Servings: 4 | Cooking Time: 15 Minutes

Ingredients:
- ½ cup vegetable oil, plus 3 tablespoons
- ¼ cup white wine vinegar
- 1 garlic clove, grated
- 2 summer squash, sliced lengthwise about ¼-inch thick
- 1 red onion, peeled and cut into wedges
- Sea salt, to taste
- Freshly ground black pepper, to taste
- 1 package crumbled feta cheese
- Red pepper flakes, as needed

Directions:
1. Insert the Grill Grate and close the hood. Select GRILL, set the temperature to MAX, and set the time to 15 minutes. Select START/STOP to begin preheating.
2. Meanwhile, in a small bowl, whisk together ½ cup oil, vinegar, and garlic, and set aside.
3. In a large bowl, toss the squash and onion with remaining 3 tablespoons of oil until evenly coated. Season with the salt and pepper.
4. When the unit beeps to signify it has preheated, arrange the squash and onions on the Grill Grate. Close the hood and GRILL for 6 minutes.
5. After 6 minutes, open the hood and flip the squash. Close the hood and GRILL for 6 to 9 minutes more.
6. When vegetables are cooked to desired doneness, remove them from the grill. Arrange the vegetables on a large platter and top with the feta cheese. Drizzle the dressing over the top, and sprinkle with the red pepper flakes. Let stand for 15 minutes before serving.

Cayenne Sesame Nut Mix

Servings:4 | Cooking Time: 2 Minutes

Ingredients:
- 1 tablespoon buttery spread, melted
- 2 teaspoons honey
- ¼ teaspoon cayenne pepper
- 2 teaspoons sesame seeds
- ¼ teaspoon kosher salt
- ¼ teaspoon freshly ground black pepper
- 1 cup cashews
- 1 cup almonds
- 1 cup mini pretzels
- 1 cup rice squares cereal
- Cooking spray

Directions:
1. Select BAKE, set the temperature to 360°F, and set the time to 2 minutes. Select START/STOP to begin pre-heating.
2. In a large bowl, combine the buttery spread, honey, cayenne pepper, sesame seeds, kosher salt, and black pepper, then add the cashews, almonds, pretzels, and rice squares, tossing to coat.
3. Spray a baking pan with cooking spray, then pour the mixture into the pan. Place the pan directly in the pot. Close the hood and BAKE for 2 minutes.
4. Remove the sesame mix from the grill and allow to cool in the pan on a wire rack for 5 minutes before serving.

Roasted Mixed Nuts

Servings: 6 | Cooking Time: 20 Minutes

Ingredients:
- 2 cups mixed nuts (walnuts, pecans, and almonds)
- 2 tablespoons egg white
- 2 tablespoons sugar
- 1 teaspoon paprika
- 1 teaspoon ground cinnamon
- Cooking spray

Directions:
1. Spray the Crisper Basket with cooking spray.
2. Insert the Crisper Basket and close the hood. Select ROAST, set the temperature to 300°F, and set the time to 20 minutes. Select START/STOP to begin preheating.
3. Stir together the mixed nuts, egg white, sugar, paprika, and cinnamon in a small bowl until the nuts are fully coated.
4. Put the nuts in the Crisper Basket. Close the hood and ROAST for 20 minutes. Shake the basket halfway through the cooking time for even cooking.
5. Transfer the nuts to a bowl and serve warm.

Grilled Blooming Onion

Servings: 4 | Cooking Time: 12 Minutes

Ingredients:
- 2 large yellow onions
- 1 cup milk
- 2 large eggs
- 1 teaspoon paprika
- 1 teaspoon cayenne pepper
- 1 teaspoon garlic powder
- 1 teaspoon onion powder
- 2 cups all-purpose flour
- Salt
- Freshly ground black pepper
- Nonstick cooking spray

Directions:
1. Insert the Grill Grate and close the hood. Select GRILL, set the temperature to LO, and set the time to 12 minutes. Select START/STOP to begin preheating.
2. While the unit is preheating, cut off both ends of the onions, keeping the root end as intact as possible. Peel off the outer layer of skin. With the root facing up, begin cutting your petals Starting from ¼ inch below the root end (do not cut through the root), cut downward to slit the onion into 4 equal sections, and then again in between each cut so there are 8 equal sections, and then again to make 16 petals. Turn the onion upside down so the root is now on the bottom, and the petals should begin to open.
3. In a large bowl, whisk together the milk and eggs. Carefully place the blooming onion in the mixture to soak.
4. In a separate large bowl, combine the paprika, cayenne pepper, garlic powder, onion powder, and flour. Season with salt and pepper. Transfer the blooming onion to the bowl with the seasonings. Using your hands, carefully sift some of the mixture into the cracks of the onion, making sure the petals are coated well. Shake off any excess.
5. When the unit beeps to signify it has preheated, generously spray the onion with cooking spray and place it, petals facing up, on the Grill Grate. Close the hood and grill for 10 minutes.
6. After 10 minutes, open the hood and check for crispiness and if the onion is browned to your liking. To continue cooking, generously spray the onion with more cooking spray. Close the hood and continue cooking for 2 minutes more, or until the onions have browned and crisped up to your desired doneness. Remove the onion from the grill and serve.

Avocado Egg Rolls

Servings: 4 | Cooking Time: 10 Minutes

Ingredients:
- 4 avocados, pitted and diced
- ½ white onion, diced
- ⅓ cup sun-dried tomatoes, chopped
- 1 (16-ounce) package egg roll wrappers (about 20 wrappers)
- ¼ cup water, for sealing
- 4 tablespoons avocado oil

Directions:
1. Insert the Grill Grate and close the hood. Select GRILL, set the temperature to LO, and set the time to 10 minutes. Select START/STOP to begin preheating.
2. While the unit is preheating, place the diced avocado in a large bowl. Add the onion and sun-dried tomatoes and gently fold together, being careful to not mash the avocado.
3. Place an egg roll wrapper on a flat surface with a corner facing you (like a diamond). Add 2 to 3 tablespoons of the filling in the center of the wrapper. The amount should be about 2½ inches wide. Gently lift the bottom corner of the wrapper over the filling, fold in the sides, and roll away from you to close. Dip your finger into the water and run it over the top corner of the wrapper to seal it. Continue filling, folding, and sealing the rest of the egg rolls.
4. When the unit beeps to signify it has preheated, brush the avocado oil on all sides of the egg rolls. Place the egg rolls on the Grill Grate, seam-side down. Close the hood and grill for 5 minutes.
5. After 5 minutes, open the hood and flip the egg rolls. Give them another brush of avocado oil. Close the hood and cook for 5 minutes more.
6. When cooking is complete, the wrappers will be golden brown. Remove from the grill and serve.

Bacon-wrapped Dates

Servings: 6 | Cooking Time: 10 To 14 Minutes

Ingredients:
- 12 dates, pitted
- 6 slices high-quality bacon, cut in half
- Cooking spray

Directions:
1. Insert the Crisper Basket and close the hood. Select BAKE, set the temperature to 360°F, and set the time to 7 minutes. Select START/STOP to begin preheating.
2. Wrap each date with half a bacon slice and secure with a toothpick.
3. Spray the Crisper Basket with cooking spray, then place 6 bacon-wrapped dates in the basket. Place the pan directly in the pot. Close the hood and BAKE for 5 to 7 minutes or until the bacon is crispy. Repeat this process with the remaining dates.
4. Remove the dates and allow to cool on a wire rack for 5 minutes before serving.

Turkey Bacon-wrapped Dates

Servings:16 | Cooking Time: 5 To 7 Minutes

Ingredients:
- 16 whole dates, pitted
- 16 whole almonds
- 6 to 8 strips turkey bacon, cut in half

Directions:
1. Insert the Crisper Basket and close the hood. Select AIR CRISP, set the temperature to 390°F, and set the time to 7 minutes. Select START/STOP to begin preheating.
2. On a flat work surface, stuff each pitted date with a whole almond.
3. Wrap half slice of bacon around each date and secure it with a toothpick.
4. Place the bacon-wrapped dates in the Crisper Basket. Close the hood and AIR CRISP for 5 to 7 minutes, or until the bacon is cooked to your desired crispiness.
5. Transfer the dates to a paper towel-lined plate to drain. Serve hot.

Bruschetta With Tomato And Basil

Servings: 6 | Cooking Time: 6 Minutes

Ingredients:
- 4 tomatoes, diced
- ⅓ cup shredded fresh basil
- ¼ cup shredded Parmesan cheese
- 1 tablespoon balsamic vinegar
- 1 tablespoon minced garlic
- 1 teaspoon olive oil
- 1 teaspoon salt
- 1 teaspoon freshly ground black pepper
- 1 loaf French bread, cut into 1-inch-thick slices
- Cooking spray

Directions:
1. Insert the Crisper Basket and close the hood. Select BAKE, set the temperature to 250°F, and set the time to 3 minutes. Select START/STOP to begin preheating.
2. Mix together the tomatoes and basil in a medium bowl. Add the cheese, vinegar, garlic, olive oil, salt, and pepper and stir until well incorporated. Set aside.
3. Spritz the Crisper Basket with cooking spray. Working in batches, lay the bread slices in the basket in a single layer. Spray the slices with cooking spray.
4. Close the hood and BAKE for 3 minutes until golden brown.
5. Remove from the basket to a plate. Repeat with the remaining bread slices.
6. Top each slice with a generous spoonful of the tomato mixture and serve.

Twice Air-crisped Potatoes

Servings: 4 | Cooking Time: 40 Minutes

Ingredients:
- 4 medium Idaho or russet potatoes
- Extra-virgin olive oil
- Kosher salt
- 8 tablespoons (1 stick) unsalted butter, at room temperature
- ½ cup sour cream
- 1 cup shredded cheddar cheese
- Freshly ground black pepper

Directions:
1. Insert the Crisper Basket and close the hood. Select AIR CRISP, set the temperature to 400°F, and set the time to 40 minutes. Select START/STOP to begin preheating.
2. While the unit is preheating, rinse and scrub the potatoes. Poke each potato several times with a fork. Brush a generous amount of olive oil over the potatoes and season well with salt.
3. When the unit beeps to signify it has preheated, place the potatoes in the Crisper Basket. Close the hood and cook for 30 minutes.
4. After 30 minutes, open the hood and remove the potatoes. Place on a plate and set aside.
5. Slice the potatoes in half lengthwise. Use a fork to carefully scoop out the insides of the potatoes without damaging the skins. Put the potato flesh in a large bowl. Add the butter, sour cream, and cheddar cheese. Using a spatula, carefully fold the mixture until the butter melts. Scoop the filling into the potato skins. Season each potato half with salt and pepper.
6. Place the loaded potatoes back into the Crisper Basket. Close the hood and cook for 10 minutes more.
7. When cooking is complete, the potato skins will be crispy and the cheese will be melted and infused into the potatoes. Remove the potatoes from the grill and serve.

Cheese And Ham Stuffed Baby Bella

Servings: 8 | Cooking Time: 12 Minutes

Ingredients:
- 4 ounces Mozzarella cheese, cut into pieces
- ½ cup diced ham
- 2 green onions, chopped
- 2 tablespoons bread crumbs
- ½ teaspoon garlic powder
- ¼ teaspoon ground oregano
- ¼ teaspoon ground black pepper
- 1 to 2 teaspoons olive oil
- 16 fresh Baby Bella mushrooms, stemmed removed

Directions:
1. Process the cheese, ham, green onions, bread crumbs, garlic powder, oregano, and pepper in a food processor until finely chopped.
2. With the food processor running, slowly drizzle in 1 to 2 teaspoons olive oil until a thick paste has formed. Transfer the mixture to a bowl.
3. Evenly divide the mixture into the mushroom caps and lightly press down the mixture.
4. Insert the Crisper Basket and close the hood. Select ROAST, set the temperature to 390ºF, and set the time to 12 minutes. Select START/STOP to begin preheating.
5. Lay the mushrooms in the Crisper Basket in a single layer. You'll need to work in batches to avoid overcrowding.
6. Close the hood and ROAST for 12 minutes until the mushrooms are lightly browned and tender.
7. Remove from the basket to a plate and repeat with the remaining mushrooms.
8. Let the mushrooms cool for 5 minutes and serve warm.

Goat Cheese Bruschetta With Tomatoes

Servings: 4 | Cooking Time: 8 Minutes

Ingredients:
- 8 ounces cherry tomatoes (about 35)
- 8 fresh basil leaves
- 1 tablespoon balsamic vinegar
- 1 (8-ounce) baguette
- ½ cup extra-virgin olive oil
- 2 tablespoons garlic powder
- 8 ounces goat cheese (unflavored)

Directions:
1. Insert the Grill Grate and close the hood. Select GRILL, set the temperature to HI, and set the time to 8 minutes. Select START/STOP to begin preheating.
2. While the unit is preheating, quarter the cherry tomatoes. Slice the basil leaves into very thin ribbons. Place the tomatoes and basil in a medium bowl. Add the balsamic vinegar and toss to coat.
3. Slice the baguette into ½-inch slices. In a small bowl, whisk together the olive oil and garlic powder. Brush both sides of the baguette slices with the olive oil mixture.
4. When the unit beeps to signify it has preheated, place half the baguette slices on the Grill Grate in a single layer. Close the hood and cook for 4 minutes. After 4 minutes, remove the baguettes from the grill and set aside on a plate. Place the remaining slices on the Grill Grate. Close the hood and cook for 4 minutes.
5. When cooking is complete, spread a layer of goat cheese on the baguette slices. Top with the tomato-basil mixture and serve.

Maple Butter Corn Bread

Servings: 4 | Cooking Time: 40 Minutes

Ingredients:
- For the corn bread
- 1 cup all-purpose flour
- 1 cup yellow cornmeal
- 2 teaspoons baking powder
- 1 teaspoon salt
- 1¼ cups milk
- ⅓ cup canola oil
- 1 large egg
- 1 (14.75-ounce) can cream-style sweet corn
- Cooking spray
- For the maple butter
- 1 tablespoon light brown sugar, packed
- 1 tablespoon milk
- 8 tablespoons (1 stick) unsalted butter, at room temperature
- 1 tablespoon maple syrup

Directions:

1. Insert the Cooking Pot and close the hood. Select BAKE, set the temperature to 350°F, and set the time to 40 minutes. Select START/STOP to begin preheating.

2. While the unit is preheating, in a large bowl, combine the flour, cornmeal, baking powder, salt, milk, oil, egg, and sweet corn. Mix until just combined. Grease a 9-by-5-inch loaf pan with cooking spray and pour in the corn bread batter.

3. When the unit beeps to signify it has preheated, place the pan in the Cooking Pot. Close the hood and cook for 40 minutes. If using a metal loaf pan, check the corn bread after 30 minutes, as metal pans may cook faster than glass. Bake until golden brown and the mix is completely baked through.

4. When cooking is complete, the corn bread should be golden brown and a toothpick inserted into the center of the corn bread comes out clean. Remove the pan from the grill and set aside to cool.

5. In a small bowl, whisk together the brown sugar and milk until the sugar is dissolved. Add the butter and continue whisking. Add the maple syrup and continue whisking until fully combined.

6. Cut the corn bread into slices, top with the butter, and serve.

Blt With Grilled Heirloom Tomato

Servings: 4 | Cooking Time: 10 Minutes

Ingredients:
- 8 slices white bread
- 8 tablespoons mayonnaise
- 2 heirloom tomatoes, sliced ¼-inch thick
- 2 tablespoons canola oil
- Sea salt, to taste
- Freshly ground black pepper, to taste
- 8 slices bacon, cooked
- 8 leaves iceberg lettuce

Directions:

1. Insert the Grill Grate, and close the hood. Select GRILL, set the temperature to MAX, and set the time to 10 minutes. Select START/STOP to begin preheating.

2. While the unit is preheating, spread a thin layer of mayonnaise on one side of each piece of bread.

3. When the unit beeps to signify it has preheated, place the bread, mayonnaise-side down, on the Grill Grate. Close the hood and GRILL for 2 to 3 minutes, until crisp.

4. Meanwhile, remove the watery pulp and seeds from the tomato slices. Brush both sides of the tomatoes with the oil and season with salt and pepper.

5. After 2 to 3 minutes, remove the bread and place the tomatoes on the grill. Close the hood and continue grilling for the remaining 6 to 8 minutes.

6. To assemble, spread a thin layer of mayonnaise on the non-grilled sides of the bread. Layer the tomatoes, bacon, and lettuce on the bread, and top with the remaining slices of bread. Slice each sandwich in half and serve.

Balsamic Broccoli

Servings: 4 | Cooking Time: 10 Minutes

Ingredients:

- 4 tablespoons soy sauce
- 4 tablespoons balsamic vinegar
- 2 tablespoons canola oil
- 2 teaspoons maple syrup
- 2 heads broccoli, trimmed into florets
- Red pepper flakes, for garnish
- Sesame seeds, for garnish

Directions:

1. Insert the Grill Grate and close the hood. Select GRILL, set the temperature to MAX, and set the time to 10 minutes. Select START/STOP to begin preheating.
2. While the unit is preheating, in a large bowl, whisk together the soy sauce, balsamic vinegar, oil, and maple syrup. Add the broccoli and toss to coat evenly.
3. When the unit beeps to signify it has preheated, place the broccoli on the Grill Grate. Close the hood and GRILL for 8 to 10 minutes, until charred on all sides.
4. When cooking is complete, place the broccoli on a large serving platter. Garnish with red pepper flakes and sesame seeds. Serve immediately.

Garlicky And Lemony Artichokes

Servings: 4 | Cooking Time: 10 Minutes

Ingredients:

- Juice of ½ lemon
- ½ cup canola oil
- 3 garlic cloves, chopped
- Sea salt, to taste
- Freshly ground black pepper, to taste
- 2 large artichokes, trimmed and halved

Directions:

1. Insert the Grill Grate and close the hood. Select GRILL, set the temperature to MAX, and set the time to 10 minutes. Select START/STOP to begin preheating.
2. While the unit is preheating, in a medium bowl, combine the lemon juice, oil, and garlic. Season with salt and pepper, then brush the artichoke halves with the lemon-garlic mixture.
3. When the unit beeps to signify it has preheated, place the artichokes on the Grill Grate, cut side down. Gently press them down to maximize grill marks. Close the hood and GRILL for 8 to 10 minutes, occasionally basting generously with the lemon-garlic mixture throughout cooking, until blistered on all sides.

Zucchini And Potato Tots

Servings: 4 | Cooking Time: 20 Minutes

Ingredients:

- 1 large zucchini, grated
- 1 medium baked potato, skin removed and mashed
- ¼ cup shredded Cheddar cheese
- 1 large egg, beaten
- ½ teaspoon kosher salt
- Cooking spray

Directions:

1. Select AIR CRISP, set the temperature to 390ºF, and set the time to 10 minutes. Select START/STOP to begin preheating.
2. Wrap the grated zucchini in a paper towel and squeeze out any excess liquid, then combine the zucchini, baked potato, shredded Cheddar cheese, egg, and kosher salt in a large bowl.
3. Spray a baking pan with cooking spray, then place individual tablespoons of the zucchini mixture in the pan. Place the pan directly in the pot. Close the hood and AIR CRISP for 10 minutes. Repeat this process with the remaining mixture.
4. Remove the tots and allow to cool on a wire rack for 5 minutes before serving.

Garlic Fries

Servings: 4 | Cooking Time: 20 Minutes

Ingredients:
- 2 large Idaho or russet potatoes (1½ to 2 pounds)
- 1 head garlic (10 to 12 cloves)
- 4 tablespoons avocado oil, divided
- 1 teaspoon sea salt
- Chopped fresh parsley, for garnish

Directions:

1. Cut the potatoes into ¼-inch-thick slices. Place the slices in a large bowl and cover with cold water. Set aside for 30 minutes. This will ensure the potatoes cook well and crisp up perfectly. While the potatoes are soaking, mince the garlic cloves.
2. Drain the potatoes and pat dry using paper towels. In a large bowl, toss the potato slices with 2 tablespoons of avocado oil.
3. Insert the Cooking Pot and Crisper Basket and close the hood. Select AIR CRISP, set the temperature to 390°F, and set the time to 20 minutes. Select START/STOP to begin preheating.
4. While the unit is preheating, in a small bowl, combine the remaining 2 tablespoons of avocado oil with the minced garlic.
5. When the unit beeps to signify it has preheated, put the fries in the Crisper Basket. Close the hood and cook for 10 minutes.
6. After 10 minutes, open the hood and give the basket a shake to toss the fries. Close the hood and continue cooking for 5 minutes. Open the hood again and give the basket a shake. Close the hood and cook for 5 minutes more.
7. When cooking is complete, the fries will be crispy and golden brown. If you like them extra-crispy, continue cooking to your liking. Transfer the fries to a large bowl and drizzle with the garlic oil. Toss and season with the salt. Garnish with the parsley and serve.

Herbed Pita Chips

Servings: 4 | Cooking Time: 5 To 6 Minutes

Ingredients:
- ¼ teaspoon dried basil
- ¼ teaspoon marjoram
- ¼ teaspoon ground oregano
- ¼ teaspoon garlic powder
- ¼ teaspoon ground thyme
- ¼ teaspoon salt
- 2 whole 6-inch pitas, whole grain or white
- Cooking spray

Directions:

1. Insert the Crisper Basket and close the hood. Select BAKE, set the temperature to 330°F, and set the time to 6 minutes. Select START/STOP to begin preheating.
2. Mix all the seasonings together.
3. Cut each pita half into 4 wedges. Break apart wedges at the fold.
4. Mist one side of pita wedges with oil. Sprinkle with half of seasoning mix.
5. Turn pita wedges over, mist the other side with oil, and sprinkle with remaining seasonings.
6. Place pita wedges in Crisper Basket. Close the hood and BAKE for 2 minutes.
7. Shake the basket and bake for 2 minutes longer. Shake again, and if needed, bake for 1 or 2 more minutes, or until crisp. Watch carefully because at this point they will cook very quickly.
8. Serve hot.

Sweet Potato Chips

Servings:1 | Cooking Time: 8 To 10 Hours

Ingredients:
- 1 sweet potato, peeled
- ½ tablespoon avocado oil
- ½ teaspoon sea salt

Directions:
1. Using a mandoline, thinly slice (⅛ inch or less) the sweet potato.
2. In a large bowl, toss the sweet potato slices with the oil until evenly coated. Season with the salt.
3. Place the sweet potato slices flat on the Crisper Basket. Arrange them in a single layer, without any slices touching each another.
4. Place the basket in the pot and close the hood.
5. Select DEHYDRATE, set the temperature to 120°F, and set the time to 10 hours. Select START/STOP.
6. After 8 hours, check for desired doneness. Continue dehydrating for 2 more hours, if necessary.
7. When cooking is complete, remove the basket from the pot. Transfer the sweet potato chips to an airtight container and store at room temperature.

Brussels Sprouts And Bacon

Servings: 4 | Cooking Time: 12 Minutes

Ingredients:
- 1 pound Brussels sprouts, trimmed and halved
- 2 tablespoons extra-virgin olive oil
- 1 teaspoon sea salt
- ½ teaspoon freshly ground black pepper
- 6 slices bacon, chopped

Directions:
1. Insert the Crisper Basket and close the hood. Select AIR CRISP, set the temperature to 390°F, and set the time to 12 minutes. Select START/STOP to begin preheating.
2. Meanwhile, in a large bowl, toss the Brussels sprouts with the olive oil, salt, pepper, and bacon.
3. When the unit beeps to signify it has preheated, add the Brussels sprouts to the basket. Close the hood and AIR CRISP for 10 minutes.
4. After 6 minutes, shake the basket of Brussels sprouts. Place the basket back in the unit and close the hood to resume cooking.
5. After 6 minutes, check for desired crispness. Continue cooking up to 2 more minutes, if necessary.

Crispy Prosciutto-wrapped Asparagus

Servings: 6 | Cooking Time: 16 To 24 Minutes

Ingredients:
- 12 asparagus spears, woody ends trimmed
- 24 pieces thinly sliced prosciutto
- Cooking spray

Directions:
1. Insert the Crisper Basket and close the hood. Select AIR CRISP, set the temperature to 360°F, and set the time to 4 minutes. Select START/STOP to begin preheating.
2. Wrap each asparagus spear with 2 slices of prosciutto, then repeat this process with the remaining asparagus and prosciutto.
3. Spray the Crisper Basket with cooking spray, then place 2 to 3 bundles in the basket. Close the hood and AIR CRISP for 4 minutes. Repeat this process with the remaining asparagus bundles.
4. Remove the bundles and allow to cool on a wire rack for 5 minutes before serving.

SEAFOOD

SEAFOOD

Chili-lime Shrimp Skewers

Servings: 4 | Cooking Time: 10 Minutes

Ingredients:

- 2 pounds jumbo shrimp, peeled
- 1 tablespoon chili powder
- ¼ teaspoon ground cumin
- ¼ teaspoon dried oregano
- ¼ teaspoon garlic powder
- 2 tablespoons honey
- Juice of 2 limes, divided
- Instant rice, prepared as directed

Directions:

1. Insert the Grill Grate and close the hood. Select GRILL, set the temperature to HI, and set the time to 5 minutes. Select START/STOP to begin preheating.
2. While the unit is preheating, thread 4 or 5 shrimp onto each of 8 skewers, leaving about an inch of space at the bottom. Place the skewers on a large plate.
3. In a small bowl, combine the chili powder, cumin, oregano, and garlic powder. Lightly coat the shrimp with the dry rub. In the same bowl, add the honey and the juice of ½ lime to any remaining seasoning. Mix together.
4. When the unit beeps to signify it has preheated, place 4 shrimp skewers on the Grill Grate. Brush the shrimp with some of the honey mixture. Close the hood and grill for 2 minutes, 30 seconds.
5. After 2 minutes, 30 seconds, open the hood and squeeze the juice of another ½ lime over the skewers and flip. Brush on more honey mixture. Close the hood and cook for 2 minutes, 30 seconds.
6. When cooking is complete, the shrimp should be opaque and pink. Remove the skewers from the grill. Select GRILL, set the temperature to HI, and set the time to 5 minutes. Select START/STOP to begin and press PREHEAT to skip preheating. Repeat steps 4 and 5 for the remaining 4 skewers. When all of the skewers are cooked, serve with the rice.

Grilled Mahi-mahi Tacos With Spicy Coleslaw

Servings: 4 | Cooking Time: 10 Minutes

Ingredients:

- 1 teaspoon garlic powder
- 1 teaspoon onion powder
- 1 tablespoon paprika
- ¼ teaspoon salt
- 4 (8-ounce) mahi-mahi fillets
- Avocado oil
- Juice of 2 limes, divided
- 1 cup mayonnaise
- 1 tablespoon sriracha
- ⅛ teaspoon cayenne pepper
- ½ head red cabbage, shredded
- 8 (6-inch) corn tortillas

Directions:

1. Insert the Grill Grate and close the hood. Select GRILL, set the temperature to MED, and set the time to 10 minutes. Select START/STOP to begin preheating.
2. While the unit is preheating, in a small bowl, combine the garlic powder, onion powder, paprika, and salt. Place the mahi-mahi fillets on a large plate and rub avocado oil on both sides. Then squeeze the juice of 1 lime on top and generously coat the fillets with the seasoning mix.
3. When the unit beeps to signify it has preheated, place the fillets on the Grill Grate. Close the hood and grill for 8 minutes.
4. While the mahi-mahi is cooking, in a large bowl, combine the mayonnaise, sriracha, cayenne pepper, and the juice of the remaining lime. Add the shredded cabbage to the bowl and stir until combined.
5. After 8 minutes, open the hood and remove the fillets from the grill. Place the tortillas on the Grill Grate. Close the hood to warm them for 2 minutes. Feel free to flip after 1 minute, if desired.
6. Cut the mahi-mahi into ½-inch to 1-inch strips. To assemble the tacos, place the mahi-mahi pieces on the tortillas and dress with the spicy coleslaw mix. Serve.

Buttered Lobster Tails

Servings: 6 | Cooking Time: 7 Minutes

Ingredients:
- 6 (4-ounce) lobster tails
- Paprika
- Salt
- Freshly ground black pepper
- 4 tablespoons (½ stick) unsalted butter, melted
- 3 garlic cloves, minced

Directions:

1. Place the lobster tails shell-side up on a cutting board. Using kitchen shears, cut each shell down the center, stopping at the base of the tail. Carefully crack open the shell by sliding your thumbs between the shell and meat and delicately pulling apart. Wiggle, pull, and lift the meat out of the shell. Remove the vein and digestive tract, if present. Rest the meat on top of the shell for a beautiful display.

2. Insert the Grill Grate and close the hood. Select GRILL, set the temperature to HI, and set the time to 7 minutes. Select START/STOP to begin preheating.

3. While the unit is preheating, season the lobster meat with paprika, salt, and pepper.

4. In a small bowl, combine the melted butter and garlic.

5. When the unit beeps to signify it has preheated, place the lobster tails on their shells on the Grill Grate. Close the hood and grill for 4 minutes.

6. After 4 minutes, open the hood and brush the garlic butter on the lobster meat. Close the hood and cook for 3 minutes more.

7. When cooking is complete, the lobster meat will be opaque and the shell will be orangey red. Serve with more melted butter or a sauce of your choice.

Shrimp Boil

Servings: 6 | Cooking Time: 10 Minutes

Ingredients:
- 2 tablespoons lemon-pepper seasoning
- 2 tablespoons light brown sugar, packed
- 2 tablespoons minced garlic
- 2 tablespoons Old Bay seasoning
- ¼ teaspoon Cajun seasoning
- ¼ teaspoon paprika
- ¼ teaspoon cayenne pepper
- 1 teaspoon garlic powder
- 1½ cups (3 sticks) unsalted butter, cut into quarters
- 2 pounds shrimp

Directions:

1. Insert the Cooking Pot and close the hood. Select GRILL, set the temperature to MED, and set the time to 10 minutes. Select START/STOP to begin preheating.

2. While the unit is preheating, in a small bowl, combine the lemon pepper, brown sugar, minced garlic, Old Bay seasoning, Cajun seasoning, paprika, cayenne pepper, and garlic powder.

3. When the unit beeps to signify it has preheated, place the butter and the lemon-pepper mixture in the Cooking Pot. Insert the Grill Grate and place the shrimp on it in a single layer. Close the hood and grill for 5 minutes.

4. After 5 minutes, open the hood and use grill mitts to remove the Grill Grate. Place the shrimp in the Cooking Pot. Stir to combine. Close the hood and cook for 5 minutes more.

5. When cooking is complete, open the hood and stir once more. Then close the hood and let the butter set with the shrimp for 5 minutes. Serve.

Tomato-stuffed Grilled Sole

Servings: 6 | Cooking Time: 7 Minutes

Ingredients:
- 6 tablespoons mayonnaise
- 1 teaspoon garlic powder
- 1 (14-ounce) can diced tomatoes, drained
- 6 (4-ounce) sole fillets
- Cooking spray
- 6 tablespoons panko bread crumbs

Directions:

1. Insert the Grill Grate and close the hood. Select GRILL, set the temperature to HI, and set the time to 7 minutes. Select START/STOP to begin preheating.
2. While the unit is preheating, in a small bowl, combine the mayonnaise and garlic powder. Slowly fold in the tomatoes, making sure to be gentle so they don't turn to mush. Place the sole fillets on a large, flat surface and spread the mayonnaise across the top of each. Roll up the fillets, creating pinwheels. Spray the top of each roll with cooking spray, then press 1 tablespoon of panko bread crumbs on top of each.
3. When the unit beeps to signify it has preheated, place the fillets on the Grill Grate, seam-side down. Close the hood and grill for 7 minutes.
4. When cooking is complete, the panko bread crumbs will be crisp, and the fish will have turned opaque. Remove the fish from the grill and serve.

Honey-walnut Shrimp

Servings: 4 | Cooking Time: 8 Minutes

Ingredients:
- 2 ounces walnuts
- 2 tablespoons honey
- 1 egg
- 1 cup panko bread crumbs
- 1 pound shrimp, peeled
- ½ cup mayonnaise
- 1 teaspoon powdered sugar
- 2 tablespoons heavy (whipping) cream
- Scallions, both white and green parts, sliced, for garnish

Directions:

1. Insert the Grill Grate. In a small heat-safe bowl, combine the walnuts and honey, then place the bowl on the Grill Grate and close the hood. Select GRILL, set the temperature to HI, and set the time to 8 minutes. Select START/STOP to begin preheating. After 2 minutes of preheating (set a separate timer), remove the bowl. Close the hood to continue preheating.
2. While the unit is preheating, create an assembly line with 2 large bowls. In the first bowl, whisk the egg. Put the panko bread crumbs in the other bowl. One at a time, dip the shrimp in the egg and then into the panko bread crumbs until well coated. Place the breaded shrimp on a plate.
3. When the unit beeps to signify it has preheated, place the shrimp on the Grill Grate in a single layer. Close the hood and cook for 4 minutes.
4. After 4 minutes, open the hood and flip the shrimp. Close the hood and cook for 4 minutes more.
5. While the shrimp are cooking, in a large bowl, combine the mayonnaise, powdered sugar, and heavy cream and mix until the sugar has dissolved.
6. When cooking is complete, remove the shrimp from the grill. Add the cooked shrimp and honey walnuts to the mayonnaise mixture and gently fold them together. Garnish with scallions and serve.

Crab Cakes With Lemon-garlic Aioli

Servings:12 | Cooking Time: 16 Minutes

Ingredients:
- For the crab cakes
- 1 large egg
- 1 tablespoon Old Bay seasoning
- 1 tablespoon dried parsley
- 1 tablespoon soy sauce
- 1 tablespoon minced garlic
- ¼ cup grated Parmesan cheese
- ½ cup mayonnaise
- ½ cup panko bread crumbs
- 1 pound lump crabmeat
- Avocado oil cooking spray
- For the lemon-garlic aioli
- ½ cup mayonnaise
- 1 teaspoon garlic powder
- Juice of 1 lemon
- ¼ teaspoon paprika

Directions:
1. In a large bowl, whisk the egg, then add the Old Bay seasoning, parsley, soy sauce, garlic, Parmesan cheese, mayonnaise, and panko bread crumbs and mix well. Add the crabmeat and fold it in gently so the crabmeat does not fall apart. Form the mixture into 12 equal-size patties. Place the patties on a large baking sheet and refrigerate for at least 30 minutes.
2. Insert the Grill Grate and close the hood. Select Grill, set the temperature to HI, and set the time to 8 minutes. Select START/STOP to begin preheating.
3. When the unit beeps to signify it has preheated, spray avocado oil on both sides of 6 crab cakes and place them on the Grill Grate. Close the hood and cook for 4 minutes.
4. After 4 minutes, open the hood and flip the crab cakes. Close the hood and cook for 4 minutes more.
5. When cooking is complete, remove the crab cakes from the grill. Select GRILL, set the temperature to HI, and set the time to 8 minutes. Select START/STOP to begin and press PREHEAT to skip preheating. Repeat steps 3 and 4 for the remaining 6 crab cakes.
6. While the crab cakes are cooking, in a small bowl, combine the mayonnaise, garlic powder, lemon juice, and paprika. Feel free to add more lemon or a few dashes of hot sauce to adjust the taste to your liking.
7. When all of the crab cakes are cooked, serve with the sauce.

Crusted Codfish

Servings: 4 | Cooking Time: 8 Minutes

Ingredients:
- 1 cup panko bread crumbs
- 2 tablespoons grated Parmesan cheese
- ¼ cup chopped pistachios
- 4 (4-ounce) frozen cod fillets, thawed
- 4 tablespoons Dijon mustard
- Cooking spray

Directions:
1. Insert the Grill Grate and close the hood. Select GRILL, set the temperature to HI, and set the time to 8 minutes. Select START/STOP to begin preheating.
2. While the unit is preheating, on a large plate, mix together the panko bread crumbs, Parmesan cheese, and pistachios. Evenly coat both sides of the cod fillets with the mustard, then press the fillets on the panko mixture on both sides to create a crust.
3. When the unit beeps to signify it has preheated, spray the crusted fillets with cooking spray and place them on the Grill Grate. Close the hood and grill for 4 minutes.
4. After 4 minutes, open the hood and flip the fillets. Close the hood and cook for 4 minutes more.
5. When cooking is complete, remove the fillets from the grill and serve.

Lemon-garlic Butter Scallops

Servings: 6 | Cooking Time: 4 Minutes

Ingredients:
- 2 pounds large sea scallops
- Salt
- Freshly ground black pepper
- 3 tablespoons avocado oil
- 3 garlic cloves, minced
- 8 tablespoons (1 stick) unsalted butter, sliced
- Juice of 1 lemon
- Chopped fresh parsley, for garnish

Directions:
1. Insert the Cooking Pot and close the hood. Select GRILL, set the temperature to HI, and set the time to 4 minutes. Select START/STOP to begin preheating.
2. While the unit is preheating, pat the scallops dry with a paper towel and season them with salt and pepper. After 5 minutes of preheating (set a separate timer), open the hood and add the avocado oil and garlic to the Cooking Pot, then close the hood to continue preheating.
3. When the unit beeps to signify it has preheated, use a spatula to spread the oil and garlic around the bottom of the Cooking Pot. Place the scallops in the pot in a single layer. Close the hood and cook for 2 minutes.
4. After 2 minutes, open the hood and flip the scallops. Add the butter to the pot and drizzle some lemon juice over each scallop. Close the hood and cook for 2 minutes more.
5. When cooking is complete, open the hood and flip the scallops again. Spoon melted garlic butter on top of each. The scallops should be slightly firm and opaque. Remove the scallops from the grill and serve, garnished with the parsley.

Garlic Butter Shrimp Kebabs

Servings: 4 | Cooking Time: 10 Minutes

Ingredients:
- 2 tablespoons unsalted butter, at room temperature
- 4 garlic cloves, minced
- 2 pounds jumbo shrimp, peeled
- 1 tablespoon garlic salt
- 1 teaspoon dried parsley

Directions:
1. Insert the Grill Grate. Place the butter and minced garlic in a heat-safe bowl, place the bowl on the Grill Grate, and close the hood. Select GRILL, set the temperature to HI, and set the time to 5 minutes. Select START/STOP to begin preheating. After 1 minute of preheating (set a separate timer), remove the bowl with the butter. Close the hood to continue preheating.
2. While the unit is preheating, place 4 or 5 shrimp on each of 8 skewers, with at least 1 inch left at the bottom. Place the skewers on a large plate. Lightly coat them with the garlic salt and parsley.
3. When the unit beeps to signify it has preheated, place 4 skewers on the Grill Grate. Brush some of the melted garlic butter on the shrimp. Close the hood and grill for 2 minutes, 30 seconds.
4. After 2 minutes, 30 seconds, open the hood and brush the shrimp with garlic butter again, then flip the skewers. Brush on more garlic butter. Close the hood and cook for 2 minutes, 30 seconds more.
5. When cooking is complete, the shrimp will be opaque and pink. Remove the skewers from the grill. Select GRILL, set the temperature to HI, and set the time to 5 minutes. Select START/STOP to begin and press PREHEAT to skip preheating. Repeat steps 3 and 4 for the remaining skewers. When all the skewers are cooked, serve.

Lobster Rolls

Servings: 4 | Cooking Time: 7 Minutes

Ingredients:
- ¼ cup mayonnaise
- Juice of ½ lemon
- ¼ teaspoon sea salt
- ⅛ teaspoon freshly ground black pepper
- 1 teaspoon dried parsley
- Dash paprika
- 1 pound frozen lobster meat, thawed, cut into 1-inch pieces
- Unsalted butter, at room temperature
- 4 sandwich rolls, such as French rolls, hoagie rolls, or large hot dog buns
- 1 lemon, cut into wedges

Directions:
1. Insert the Grill Grate and close the hood. Select GRILL, set the temperature to MED, and set the time to 7 minutes. Select START/STOP to begin preheating.
2. While the unit is preheating, in a large bowl, combine the mayonnaise, lemon juice, salt, pepper, parsley, and paprika.
3. When the unit beeps to signify it has preheated, place the lobster meat on the Grill Grate. Close the hood and grill for 4 minutes.
4. While the lobster is cooking, spread the butter on the sandwich rolls.
5. After 4 minutes, open the hood and remove the lobster meat. Set aside on a plate. Place the sandwich rolls on the grill, buttered-side down. Close the hood and grill for 2 minutes.
6. After 2 minutes, open the hood and flip the rolls. Close the hood and cook for 1 minute more.
7. When the bread is toasted and golden brown, remove it from the grill. Add the lobster meat to the mayonnaise mixture and gently fold in until well combined. Spoon the lobster meat into the sandwich rolls. Serve with the lemon wedges.

Halibut With Lemon And Capers

Servings: 4 | Cooking Time: 8 Minutes

Ingredients:
- 4 halibut steaks (at least 1 inch thick)
- Extra-virgin olive oil
- 1 lemon
- 1 cup white wine
- 3 garlic cloves, minced
- 4 tablespoons capers
- 4 tablespoons (½ stick) unsalted butter, sliced

Directions:
1. Insert the Cooking Pot and close the hood. Select GRILL, set the temperature to HI, and set the time to 8 minutes. Select START/STOP to begin preheating.
2. While the unit is preheating, drizzle the fish fillets with olive oil. Cut half the lemon into thin slices and place them on top of the fillets.
3. When the unit beeps to signify it has preheated, place the fillets in the Cooking Pot. Close the hood and cook for 4 minutes.
4. After 4 minutes, open the hood and add the white wine. Close the hood and cook for 2 minutes. After 2 minutes, open the hood and add the garlic, capers, and butter. Squeeze the juice of the remaining ½ lemon over the fish. Close the hood and cook for 2 minutes more.
5. When cooking is complete, open the hood and spoon the sauce over the fish. If the capers have not popped, give about half of them a tap with the spoon to pop them. Stir the sauce and serve with the fillets.

Coconut Shrimp With Orange Chili Sauce

Servings:44 | Cooking Time: 16 Minutes

Ingredients:
- For the coconut shrimp
- 2 large eggs
- 1 cup sweetened coconut flakes
- 1 cup panko bread crumbs
- ½ teaspoon salt
- ¼ teaspoon freshly ground black pepper
- 2 pounds jumbo shrimp, peeled
- For the orange chili sauce
- ½ cup orange marmalade
- 1 teaspoon sriracha or ¼ teaspoon red pepper flakes

Directions:
1. Insert the Grill Grate and close the hood. Select GRILL, set the temperature to HI, and set the time to 16 minutes. Select START/STOP to begin preheating.
2. While the unit is preheating, create an assembly line with 2 large bowls. In one bowl, whisk the eggs. In the other bowl, combine the coconut flakes, panko bread crumbs, salt, and pepper. One at a time, dip the shrimp in the egg and then into the coconut flakes until fully coated.
3. When the unit beeps to signify it has preheated, place half the shrimp on the Grill Grate in a single layer. Close the hood and cook for 4 minutes.
4. After 4 minutes, open the hood and flip the shrimp. Close the hood and cook for 4 minutes more. After 4 minutes, open the hood and remove the shrimp from the grill.
5. Repeat steps 3 and 4 for the remaining shrimp.
6. To make the orange chili sauce
7. In a small bowl, combine the orange marmalade and sriracha. Serve as a dipping sauce alongside the coconut shrimp.

Orange-ginger Soy Salmon

Servings: 4 | Cooking Time: 12 Minutes

Ingredients:
- ½ cup low-sodium soy sauce
- ¼ cup orange marmalade
- 3 tablespoons light brown sugar, packed
- 1 tablespoon peeled minced fresh ginger
- 1 garlic clove, minced
- 4 (8-ounce) skin-on salmon fillets

Directions:
1. In a large bowl, whisk together the soy sauce, orange marmalade, brown sugar, ginger, and garlic until the sugar is dissolved. Set aside one-quarter of the marinade in a small bowl. Place the salmon fillets skin-side down in the marinade in the large bowl.
2. Insert the Grill Grate and close the hood. Select GRILL, set the temperature to MED, and set the time to 12 minutes. Select START/STOP to begin preheating.
3. When the unit beeps to signify it has preheated, place the salmon fillets on the Grill Grate, skin-side down. Spoon the remaining marinade in the large bowl over the fillets. Close the hood and cook for 10 minutes.
4. After 10 minutes, open the hood and brush the reserved marinade in the small bowl over the fillets. Close the hood and cook for 2 minutes more.
5. When cooking is complete, the salmon will be opaque and should flake easily with a fork. (If you want, you can also use the Smart Thermometer at the end of cooking to check that the internal temperature of the salmon has reached 145°F.) Remove the fillets from the grill and serve.

Tilapia With Cilantro And Ginger

Servings: 4 | Cooking Time: 8 Minutes

Ingredients:

- Extra-virgin olive oil
- 4 (8-ounce) tilapia fillets
- 2 tablespoons soy sauce
- 1 teaspoon sesame oil
- 1 tablespoon honey
- 1 tablespoon peeled minced fresh ginger
- ½ cup chopped fresh cilantro

Directions:

1. Insert the Cooking Pot and close the hood. Select GRILL, set the temperature to HI, and set the time to 8 minutes. Select START/STOP to begin preheating.
2. While the unit is preheating, drizzle the fish fillets with olive oil.
3. When the unit beeps to signify it has preheated, place the fillets in the Cooking Pot in a single layer. Close the hood and cook for 6 minutes.
4. While the fish is cooking, in a small bowl, whisk together the soy sauce, sesame oil, honey, ginger, and cilantro.
5. After 6 minutes, open the hood and pour the sauce over the fillets. Close the hood and cook for 2 minutes more.
6. When cooking is complete, remove the fillets from the grill and serve.

Striped Bass With Sesame-ginger Scallions

Servings: 4 | Cooking Time: 8 Minutes

Ingredients:

- 4 (8-ounce) striped bass fillets
- Extra-virgin olive oil
- 2 (1-inch) pieces fresh ginger, peeled and thinly sliced
- ½ cup soy sauce
- ½ cup rice wine (mirin)
- 2 tablespoons sesame oil
- ¼ cup light brown sugar, packed
- ¼ cup water
- ¼ cup sliced scallions, both white and green parts, for garnish

Directions:

1. Insert the Cooking Pot and close the hood. Select GRILL, set the temperature to HI, and set the time to 8 minutes. Select START/STOP to begin preheating.
2. While the unit is preheating, drizzle the fish fillets with olive oil.
3. When the unit beeps to signify it has preheated, place the fillets in the Cooking Pot in a single layer. Place the ginger slices on top of the fillets. Close the hood and cook for 6 minutes.
4. While the fish is cooking, in a small bowl, whisk together the soy sauce, rice wine, sesame oil, brown sugar, and water until the sugar dissolves.
5. After 6 minutes, open the hood and pour the soy sauce mixture over the fish. Close the hood and cook for 2 minutes more.
6. When cooking is complete, open the hood and remove the fillets from the grill. Garnish with the scallions and serve.

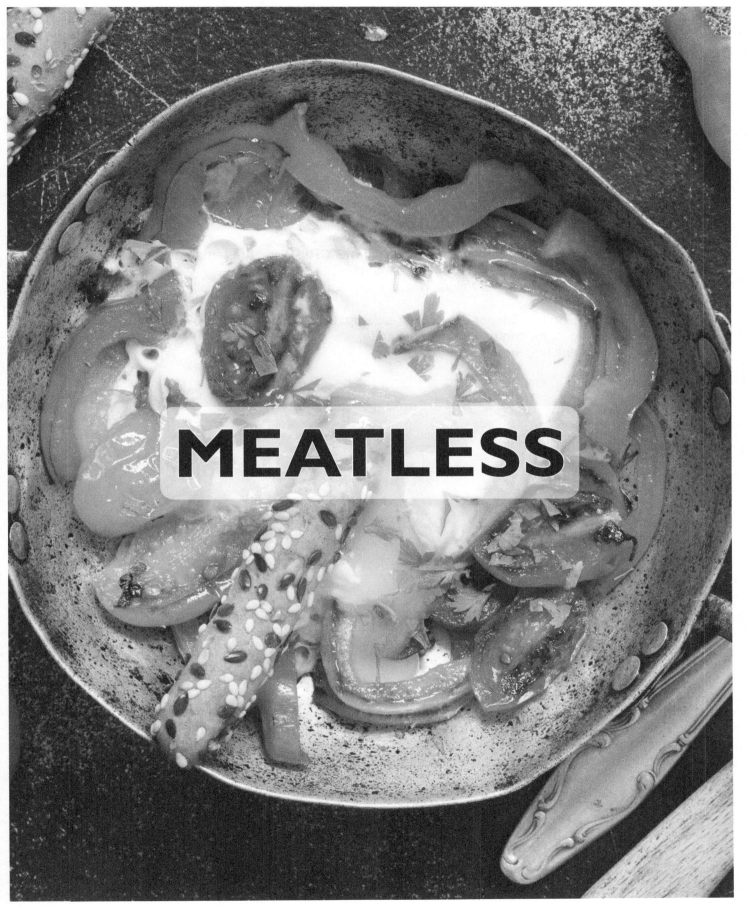

MEATLESS

MEATLESS

Cinnamon-spiced Acorn Squash

Servings: 2 | Cooking Time: 15 Minutes

Ingredients:
- 1 medium acorn squash, halved crosswise and deseeded
- 1 teaspoon coconut oil
- 1 teaspoon light brown sugar
- Few dashes of ground cinnamon
- Few dashes of ground nutmeg

Directions:
1. Insert the Crisper Basket and close the hood. Select AIR CRISP, set the temperature to 325ºF, and set the time to 15 minutes. Select START/STOP to begin preheating.
2. On a clean work surface, rub the cut sides of the acorn squash with coconut oil. Scatter with the brown sugar, cinnamon, and nutmeg.
3. Put the squash halves in the Crisper Basket, cut-side up. Close the hood and AIR CRISP for 15 minutes until just tender when pierced in the center with a paring knife.
4. Rest for 5 to 10 minutes and serve warm.

Cheesy Rice And Olives Stuffed Peppers

Servings: 4 | Cooking Time: 16 To 17 Minutes

Ingredients:
- 4 red bell peppers, tops sliced off
- 2 cups cooked rice
- 1 cup crumbled feta cheese
- 1 onion, chopped
- ¼ cup sliced kalamata olives
- ¾ cup tomato sauce
- 1 tablespoon Greek seasoning
- Salt and black pepper, to taste
- 2 tablespoons chopped fresh dill, for serving

Directions:
1. Select BAKE, set the temperature to 360ºF, and set the time to 15 minutes. Select START/STOP to begin preheating.
2. Microwave the red bell peppers for 1 to 2 minutes until tender.
3. When ready, transfer the red bell peppers to a plate to cool.
4. Mix together the cooked rice, feta cheese, onion, kalamata olives, tomato sauce, Greek seasoning, salt, and pepper in a medium bowl and stir until well combined.
5. Divide the rice mixture among the red bell peppers and transfer to a greased baking pan.
6. Place the pan directly in the pot. Close the hood and BAKE for 15 minutes, or until the rice is heated through and the vegetables are soft.
7. Remove from the basket and serve with the dill sprinkled on top.

Sesame-thyme Whole Maitake Mushrooms

Servings: 2 | Cooking Time: 15 Minutes

Ingredients:
- 1 tablespoon soy sauce
- 2 teaspoons toasted sesame oil
- 3 teaspoons vegetable oil, divided
- 1 garlic clove, minced
- 7 ounces maitake (hen of the woods) mushrooms
- ½ teaspoon flaky sea salt
- ½ teaspoon sesame seeds
- ½ teaspoon finely chopped fresh thyme leaves

Directions:
1. Insert the Crisper Basket and close the hood. Select ROAST, set the temperature to 300ºF, and set the time to 15 minutes. Select START/STOP to begin preheating.
2. Whisk together the soy sauce, sesame oil, 1 teaspoon of vegetable oil, and garlic in a small bowl.
3. Arrange the mushrooms in the Crisper Basket in a single layer. Drizzle the soy sauce mixture over the mushrooms. Close the hood and ROAST for 10 minutes.
4. Flip the mushrooms and sprinkle the sea salt, sesame seeds, and thyme leaves on top. Drizzle the remaining 2 teaspoons of vegetable oil all over. Roast for an additional 5 minutes.
5. Remove the mushrooms from the basket to a plate and serve hot.

Perfect Grilled Asparagus

Servings: 4 | Cooking Time: 6 Minutes

Ingredients:
- 24 asparagus spears, woody ends trimmed
- Extra-virgin olive oil, for drizzling
- Sea salt
- Freshly ground black pepper

Directions:
1. Insert the Grill Grate and close the hood. Select GRILL, set the temperature to HI, and set the time to 6 minutes. Select START/STOP to begin preheating.
2. While the unit is preheating, place the asparagus in a large bowl and drizzle with the olive oil. Toss to coat, then season with salt and pepper.
3. When the unit beeps to signify it has preheated, place the spears evenly spread out on the Grill Grate. Close the hood and grill for 3 minutes.
4. After 3 minutes, open the hood and flip and move the spears around. Close the hood and cook for 3 minutes more.
5. When cooking is complete, remove the asparagus from the grill and serve.

Vegetable And Cheese Stuffed Tomatoes

Servings: 4 | Cooking Time: 16 To 20 Minutes

Ingredients:
- 4 medium beefsteak tomatoes, rinsed
- ½ cup grated carrot
- 1 medium onion, chopped
- 1 garlic clove, minced
- 2 teaspoons olive oil
- 2 cups fresh baby spinach
- ¼ cup crumbled low-sodium feta cheese
- ½ teaspoon dried basil

Directions:
1. Select BAKE, set the temperature to 350ºF, and set the time to 20 minutes. Select START/STOP to begin preheating.
2. On your cutting board, cut a thin slice off the top of each tomato. Scoop out a ¼- to ½-inch-thick tomato pulp and place the tomatoes upside down on paper towels to drain. Set aside.
3. Stir together the carrot, onion, garlic, and olive oil in a baking pan. Place the pan directly in the pot. Close the hood and BAKE for 4 to 6 minutes, or until the carrot is crisp-tender.
4. Remove the pan from the grill and stir in the spinach, feta cheese, and basil.
5. Spoon ¼ of the vegetable mixture into each tomato and transfer the stuffed tomatoes to the pan.
6. Place the pan directly in the pot. Close the hood and BAKE for 12 to 14 minutes, or until the filling is hot and the tomatoes are lightly caramelized.
7. Let the tomatoes cool for 5 minutes and serve.

Cheese And Spinach Stuffed Portobellos

Servings: 4 | Cooking Time: 8 Minutes

Ingredients:
- 4 large portobello mushrooms, rinsed, stemmed, and gills removed
- 4 ounces cream cheese, at room temperature
- ½ cup mayonnaise
- ½ cup sour cream
- 1 teaspoon onion powder
- ¼ teaspoon garlic powder
- ¼ cup grated Parmesan cheese
- ½ cup shredded mozzarella cheese
- 2 cups fresh spinach

Directions:
1. Insert the Grill Grate and close the hood. Select GRILL, set the temperature to HI, and set the time to 8 minutes. Select START/STOP to begin preheating.
2. When the unit beeps to signify it has preheated, place the mushrooms on the Grill Grate, cap-side up. Close the hood and cook for 4 minutes.
3. While the mushrooms are grilling, in a large bowl, combine the cream cheese, mayonnaise, sour cream, onion powder, garlic powder, Parmesan cheese, mozzarella cheese, and spinach. Mix well.
4. After 4 minutes, open the hood and flip the mushrooms. Evenly distribute the filling inside the caps. Close the hood and cook for 4 minutes more.
5. When cooking is complete, remove the stuffed mushrooms from the grill and serve.

Veggie Taco Pie

Servings: 4 | Cooking Time: 15 Minutes

Ingredients:
- 1 (15-ounce) can pinto beans, drained and rinsed
- 1 tablespoon chili powder
- 2 teaspoons ground cumin
- 2 teaspoons sea salt
- 1 teaspoon paprika
- ½ teaspoon garlic powder
- ½ teaspoon onion powder
- ½ teaspoon dried oregano
- 4 small flour tortillas
- 1 cup sour cream
- 1 (14-ounce) can diced tomatoes, drained
- 1 (15-ounce) can black beans, drained and rinsed
- 2 cups shredded cheddar cheese

Directions:
1. Insert the Cooking Pot and close the hood. Select BAKE, set the temperature to 350°F, and set the time to 15 minutes. Select START/STOP to begin preheating.
2. While the unit is preheating, in a large bowl, mash the pinto beans with a fork. Add the chili powder, cumin, salt, paprika, garlic powder, onion powder, and oregano and mix until well combined. Place a tortilla in the bottom of a 6-inch springform pan. Spread a quarter of the mashed pinto beans on the tortilla in an even layer, then layer on a quarter each of the sour cream, tomatoes, black beans, and cheddar cheese in that order. Repeat the layers three more times, ending with cheese.
3. When the unit beeps to signify it has preheated, place the pan in the Cooking Pot. Close the hood and cook for 15 minutes.
4. When cooking is complete, the cheese will be melted. Remove the pan from the grill and serve.

Asian-inspired Broccoli
Servings: 2 | Cooking Time: 10 Minutes

Ingredients:
- 12 ounces broccoli florets
- 2 tablespoons Asian hot chili oil
- 1 teaspoon ground Sichuan peppercorns (or black pepper)
- 2 garlic cloves, finely chopped
- 1 piece fresh ginger, peeled and finely chopped
- Kosher salt and freshly ground black pepper

Directions:
1. Insert the Crisper Basket and close the hood. Select ROAST, set the temperature to 375ºF, and set the time to 10 minutes. Select START/STOP to begin preheating.
2. Toss the broccoli florets with the chili oil, Sichuan peppercorns, garlic, ginger, salt, and pepper in a mixing bowl until thoroughly coated.
3. Transfer the broccoli florets to the Crisper Basket. Close the hood and ROAST for 10 minutes, shaking the basket halfway through, or until the broccoli florets are lightly browned and tender.
4. Remove the broccoli from the basket and serve on a plate.

Double "egg" Plant (eggplant Omelets)
Servings: 4 | Cooking Time: 16 Minutes

Ingredients:
- 4 Chinese eggplants
- 2 large eggs
- Garlic powder
- Salt
- Freshly ground black pepper
- ¼ cup ketchup
- 1 tablespoon hot sauce (optional)

Directions:
1. Insert the Grill Grate. Select GRILL, set the temperature to HI, and set the time to 10 minutes. Select START/STOP to begin preheating.
2. When the unit beeps to signify it has preheated, place the whole eggplants on the Grill Grate. Close the hood and cook for 5 minutes.
3. After 5 minutes, open the hood and flip the eggplants. Close the hood and cook for 5 minutes more.
4. When cooking is complete, the eggplant skin will be charred and cracked and the flesh will be soft. Remove the eggplants from the grill and set aside to cool.
5. Once the eggplants have cooled down, peel the skin. Then, using a fork, flatten the eggplants with a brushing motion until they become pear shaped and about the thickness of a pancake.
6. Select GRILL, set the temperature to HI, and set the time to 6 minutes. Select START/STOP to begin preheating.
7. While the unit is preheating, in a large bowl, whisk the eggs. Dip each eggplant into the egg mixture to coat both sides, then season both sides with garlic powder, salt, and pepper.
8. When the grill beeps to signify it has preheated, place the coated eggplants on the Grill Grate. Close the hood and grill for 3 minutes.
9. After 3 minutes, open the hood and flip the eggplants. Close the hood and cook for 3 minutes more. Add more time if needed until you get your desired crispiness of the omelets.
10. When cooking is complete, remove the eggplant omelets from the grill. In a small bowl, combine the ketchup and hot sauce (if using), or just use ketchup if you do not like spice, and serve alongside the omelets for dipping.

Roasted Butternut Squash

Servings: 6 To 8 | Cooking Time: 40 Minutes

Ingredients:
- 2 butternut squash
- Avocado oil, for drizzling
- Salt
- Freshly ground black pepper

Directions:
1. Cut off the stem end of each squash, then cut the squash in half lengthwise. To do this, carefully rock the knife back and forth to cut through the tough skin and flesh. Use a spoon to scrape out the seeds from each half.
2. Insert the Cooking Pot and close the hood. Select ROAST, set the temperature to 400°F, and set the time to 40 minutes. Select START/STOP to begin preheating.
3. While the unit is preheating, drizzle the avocado oil over the butternut squash flesh. I also like to rub it in with my hands. Season with salt and pepper.
4. When the unit beeps to signify it has preheated, place the butternut squash in the Cooking Pot, cut-side down. Close the hood and cook for 40 minutes.
5. When cooking is complete, the flesh will be soft and easy to scoop out with a spoon. Remove from the grill and serve.

Chermoula Beet Roast

Servings: 4 | Cooking Time: 25 Minutes

Ingredients:
- Chermoula:
- 1 cup packed fresh cilantro leaves
- ½ cup packed fresh parsley leaves
- 6 cloves garlic, peeled
- 2 teaspoons smoked paprika
- 2 teaspoons ground cumin
- 1 teaspoon ground coriander
- ½ to 1 teaspoon cayenne pepper
- Pinch of crushed saffron (optional)
- ½ cup extra-virgin olive oil
- Kosher salt, to taste
- Beets:
- 3 medium beets, trimmed, peeled, and cut into 1-inch chunks
- 2 tablespoons chopped fresh cilantro
- 2 tablespoons chopped fresh parsley

Directions:
1. In a food processor, combine the cilantro, parsley, garlic, paprika, cumin, coriander, and cayenne. Pulse until coarsely chopped. Add the saffron, if using, and process until combined. With the food processor running, slowly add the olive oil in a steady stream; process until the sauce is uniform. Season with salt.
2. Insert the Crisper Basket and close the hood. Select ROAST, set the temperature to 375ºF, and set the time to 25 minutes. Select START/STOP to begin preheating.
3. In a large bowl, drizzle the beets with ½ cup of the chermoula to coat. Arrange the beets in the Crisper Basket. Close the hood and ROAST for 25 minutes, or until the beets are tender.
4. Transfer the beets to a serving platter. Sprinkle with the chopped cilantro and parsley and serve.

Cheesy Macaroni Balls

Servings: 2 | Cooking Time: 10 Minutes

Ingredients:

- 2 cups leftover macaroni
- 1 cup shredded Cheddar cheese
- ½ cup flour
- 1 cup bread crumbs
- 3 large eggs
- 1 cup milk
- ½ teaspoon salt
- ¼ teaspoon black pepper

Directions:

1. Insert the Crisper Basket and close the hood. Select AIR CRISP, set the temperature to 365°F, and set the time to 10 minutes. Select START/STOP to begin preheating.
2. In a bowl, combine the leftover macaroni and shredded cheese.
3. Pour the flour in a separate bowl. Put the bread crumbs in a third bowl. Finally, in a fourth bowl, mix the eggs and milk with a whisk.
4. With an ice-cream scoop, create balls from the macaroni mixture. Coat them the flour, then in the egg mixture, and lastly in the bread crumbs.
5. Arrange the balls in the basket. Close the hood and AIR CRISP for 10 minutes, giving them an occasional stir. Ensure they crisp up nicely.
6. Serve hot.

Corn And Potato Chowder

Servings: 4 | Cooking Time: 50 Minutes

Ingredients:

- 4 ears corn, shucked
- 2 tablespoons canola oil
- 1½ teaspoons sea salt, plus additional to season the corn
- ½ teaspoon freshly ground black pepper, plus additional to season the corn
- 3 tablespoons unsalted butter
- 1 small onion, finely chopped
- 2½ cups vegetable broth
- 1½ cups milk
- 4 cups diced potatoes
- 2 cups half-and-half
- 1½ teaspoons chopped fresh thyme

Directions:

1. Insert the Grill Grate and close the hood. Select GRILL, set the temperature to MAX, and set the time to 12 minutes. Select START/STOP to begin preheating.
2. While the unit is preheating, brush each ear of corn with ½ tablespoon of oil. Season the corn with salt and pepper to taste.
3. When the unit beeps to signify it has preheated, place the corn on the Grill Grate and close the hood. GRILL for 6 minutes.
4. After 6 minutes, flip the corn. Close the hood and continue cooking for the remaining 6 minutes.
5. When cooking is complete, remove the corn and let cool. Cut the kernels from the cobs.
6. In a food processor, purée 1 cup of corn kernels until smooth.
7. In a large pot over medium-high heat, melt the butter. Add the onion and sauté until soft, 5 to 7 minutes. Add the broth, milk, and potatoes. Bring to a simmer and cook until the potatoes are just tender, 10 to 12 minutes. Stir in the salt and pepper.
8. Stir in the puréed corn, remaining corn kernels, and half-and-half. Bring to a simmer and cook, stirring occasionally, until the potatoes are cooked through, for 15 to 20 minutes.
9. Using a potato masher or immersion blender, slightly mash some of the potatoes. Stir in the thyme, and additional salt and pepper to taste.

Fast And Easy Asparagus

Servings: 4 | Cooking Time: 5 Minutes

Ingredients:
- 1 pound fresh asparagus spears, trimmed
- 1 tablespoon olive oil
- Salt and ground black pepper, to taste

Directions:
1. Insert the Crisper Basket and close the hood. Select AIR CRISP, set the temperature to 375°F, and set the time to 5 minutes. Select START/STOP to begin preheating.
2. Combine all the ingredients and transfer to the Crisper Basket.
3. Close the hood and AIR CRISP for 5 minutes or until soft.
4. Serve hot.

Honey-glazed Roasted Veggies

Servings:3 | Cooking Time: 20 Minutes

Ingredients:
- Glaze:
- 2 tablespoons raw honey
- 2 teaspoons minced garlic
- ¼ teaspoon dried marjoram
- ¼ teaspoon dried basil
- ¼ teaspoon dried oregano
- ⅛ teaspoon dried sage
- ⅛ teaspoon dried rosemary
- ⅛ teaspoon dried thyme
- ½ teaspoon salt
- ¼ teaspoon ground black pepper
- Veggies:
- 3 to 4 medium red potatoes, cut into 1- to 2-inch pieces
- 1 small zucchini, cut into 1- to 2-inch pieces
- 1 small carrot, sliced into ¼-inch rounds
- 1 package cherry tomatoes, halved
- 1 cup sliced mushrooms
- 3 tablespoons olive oil

Directions:
1. Insert the Crisper Basket and close the hood. Select ROAST, set the temperature to 380°F, and set the time to 15 minutes. Select START/STOP to begin preheating.
2. Combine the honey, garlic, marjoram, basil, oregano, sage, rosemary, thyme, salt, and pepper in a small bowl and stir to mix well. Set aside.
3. Place the red potatoes, zucchini, carrot, cherry tomatoes, and mushroom in a large bowl. Drizzle with the olive oil and toss to coat.
4. Pour the veggies into the Crisper Basket. Close the hood and ROAST for 15 minutes, shaking the basket halfway through.
5. When ready, transfer the roasted veggies to the large bowl. Pour the honey mixture over the veggies, tossing to coat.
6. Spread out the veggies in a baking pan and place in the grill.
7. Increase the temperature to 390°F and ROAST for an additional 5 minutes, or until the veggies are tender and glazed. Serve warm.

Charred Green Beans With Sesame Seeds

Servings: 4 | Cooking Time: 8 Minutes

Ingredients:
- 1 tablespoon reduced-sodium soy sauce or tamari
- ½ tablespoon Sriracha sauce
- 4 teaspoons toasted sesame oil, divided
- 12 ounces trimmed green beans
- ½ tablespoon toasted sesame seeds

Directions:
1. Insert the Crisper Basket and close the hood. Select AIR CRISP, set the temperature to 375ºF, and set the time to 8 minutes. Select START/STOP to begin preheating.
2. Whisk together the soy sauce, Sriracha sauce, and 1 teaspoon of sesame oil in a small bowl until smooth.
3. Toss the green beans with the remaining sesame oil in a large bowl until evenly coated.
4. Place the green beans in the Crisper Basket in a single layer. You may need to work in batches to avoid overcrowding.
5. Close the hood and AIR CRISP for 8 minutes until the green beans are lightly charred and tender. Shake the basket halfway through the cooking time.
6. Remove from the basket to a platter. Repeat with the remaining green beans.
7. Pour the prepared sauce over the top of green beans and toss well. Serve sprinkled with the toasted sesame seeds.

Arugula And Broccoli Salad

Servings: 4 | Cooking Time: 12 Minutes

Ingredients:
- 2 heads broccoli, trimmed into florets
- ½ red onion, sliced
- 1 tablespoon canola oil
- 2 tablespoons extra-virgin olive oil
- 1 tablespoon freshly squeezed lemon juice
- 1 teaspoon honey
- 1 teaspoon Dijon mustard
- 1 garlic clove, minced
- Pinch red pepper flakes
- ¼ teaspoon fine sea salt
- Freshly ground black pepper, to taste
- 4 cups arugula, torn
- 2 tablespoons grated Parmesan cheese

Directions:
1. Insert the Grill Grate and close the hood. Select GRILL, set the temperature to MAX, and set the time to 12 minutes. Select START/STOP to begin preheating.
2. While the unit is preheating, in a large bowl, combine the broccoli, sliced onions, and canola oil and toss until coated.
3. When the unit beeps to signify it has preheated, place the vegetables on the Grill Grate. Close the hood and GRILL for 8 to 12 minutes, until charred on all sides.
4. Meanwhile, in a medium bowl, whisk together the olive oil, lemon juice, honey, mustard, garlic, red pepper flakes, salt, and pepper.
5. When cooking is complete, combine the roasted vegetables and arugula in a large serving bowl. Drizzle with the vinaigrette, and sprinkle with the Parmesan cheese.

Grilled Vegetable Pizza

Servings: 2 | Cooking Time: 10 Minutes

Ingredients:
- 2 tablespoons all-purpose flour, plus more as needed
- ½ store-bought pizza dough
- 1 tablespoon canola oil, divided
- ½ cup pizza sauce
- 1 cup shredded Mozzarella cheese
- ½ zucchini, thinly sliced
- ½ red onion, sliced
- ½ red bell pepper, seeded and thinly sliced

Directions:
1. Insert the Grill Grate and close the hood. Select GRILL, set the temperature to MAX, and set the time to 7 minutes. Select START/STOP to begin preheating.
2. While the unit is preheating, dust a clean work surface with the flour.
3. Place the dough on the floured surface and roll it into a 9-inch round of even thickness. Dust your rolling pin and work surface with additional flour, as needed, to ensure the dough does not stick.
4. Evenly brush the surface of the rolled-out dough with ½ tablespoon of oil. Flip the dough over and brush the other side with the remaining ½ tablespoon of oil. Poke the dough with a fork 5 or 6 times across its surface to prevent air pockets from forming while it cooks.
5. When the unit beeps to signify it has preheated, place the dough on the Grill Grate. Close the hood and GRILL for 4 minutes.
6. After 4 minutes, flip the dough, then spread the pizza sauce evenly over it. Sprinkle with the cheese, and top with the zucchini, onion, and pepper.
7. Close the hood and continue cooking for the remaining 2 to 3 minutes until the cheese is melted and the veggie slices begin to crisp.
8. When cooking is complete, let cool slightly before slicing.

Kidney Beans Oatmeal In Peppers

Servings: 2 To 4 | Cooking Time: 6 Minutes

Ingredients:
- 2 large bell peppers, halved lengthwise, deseeded
- 2 tablespoons cooked kidney beans
- 2 tablespoons cooked chick peas
- 2 cups cooked oatmeal
- 1 teaspoon ground cumin
- ½ teaspoon paprika
- ½ teaspoon salt or to taste
- ¼ teaspoon black pepper powder
- ¼ cup yogurt

Directions:
1. Insert the Crisper Basket and close the hood. Select AIR CRISP, set the temperature to 355ºF, and set the time to 6 minutes. Select START/STOP to begin preheating.
2. Put the bell peppers, cut-side down, in the Crisper Basket. Close the hood and AIR CRISP for 2 minutes.
3. Take the peppers out of the grill and let cool.
4. In a bowl, combine the rest of the ingredients.
5. Divide the mixture evenly and use each portion to stuff a pepper.
6. Return the stuffed peppers to the basket. Close the hood and AIR CRISP for 4 minutes.
7. Serve hot.

Honey-glazed Baby Carrots

Servings: 4 | Cooking Time: 12 Minutes

Ingredients:

- 1 pound baby carrots
- 2 tablespoons olive oil
- 1 tablespoon honey

- 1 teaspoon dried dill
- Salt and black pepper, to taste

Directions:

1. Insert the Crisper Basket and close the hood. Select ROAST, set the temperature to 350ºF, and set the time to 12 minutes. Select START/STOP to begin preheating.
2. Place the carrots in a large bowl. Add the olive oil, honey, dill, salt, and pepper and toss to coat well.
3. Arrange the carrots in the Crisper Basket. Close the hood and ROAST for 12 minutes, until crisp-tender. Shake the basket once during cooking.
4. Serve warm.

Black Bean And Tomato Chili

Servings: 6 | Cooking Time: 23 Minutes

Ingredients:

- 1 tablespoon olive oil
- 1 medium onion, diced
- 3 garlic cloves, minced
- 1 cup vegetable broth
- 3 cans black beans, drained and rinsed
- 2 cans diced tomatoes

- 2 chipotle peppers, chopped
- 2 teaspoons cumin
- 2 teaspoons chili powder
- 1 teaspoon dried oregano
- ½ teaspoon salt

Directions:

1. Over a medium heat, fry the garlic and onions in the olive oil for 3 minutes.
2. Add the remaining ingredients, stirring constantly and scraping the bottom to prevent sticking.
3. Select BAKE, set the temperature to 400ºF, and set the time to 20 minutes. Select START/STOP to begin preheating.
4. Take a baking pan and place the mixture inside. Put a sheet of aluminum foil on top.
5. Place the pan directly in the pot. Close the hood and BAKE for 20 minutes.
6. When ready, plate up and serve immediately.

Sweet Pepper Poppers

Servings: 4 | Cooking Time: 7 Minutes

Ingredients:

- 10 mini sweet peppers
- ½ cup mayonnaise
- 1 cup shredded sharp cheddar cheese
- ½ teaspoon onion powder
- ⅛ teaspoon cayenne powder (optional)

Directions:

1. Insert the Grill Grate and close the hood. Select GRILL, set the temperature to HI, and set the time to 7 minutes. Select START/STOP to begin preheating.
2. While the unit is preheating, cut the peppers in half lengthwise and scoop out the seeds and membranes. In a small bowl, combine the mayonnaise, cheddar cheese, onion powder, and cayenne powder (if using). Spoon the cheese mixture into each sweet pepper half.
3. When the unit beeps to signify it has preheated, place the sweet peppers on the Grill Grate, cut-side up. Close the hood and grill for 7 minutes.
4. When cooking is complete, remove the peppers from the grill and serve. Or if you prefer your peppers more charred, continue cooking to your liking.

MEATS

MEATS

Flank Steak Pinwheels

Servings: 4 To 6

Cooking Time: 10 Minutes

Ingredients:
- 2 pounds flank steak
- Salt
- Freshly ground black pepper
- 4 ounces cream cheese, at room temperature
- 2 tablespoons minced garlic
- ½ cup shredded mozzarella cheese
- 4 tablespoons grated Parmesan cheese
- 2 cups fresh spinach

Directions:
1. Insert the Grill Grate and close the hood. Select GRILL, set the temperature to HI, and set the time to 10 minutes. Select START/STOP to begin preheating.
2. While the unit is preheating, butterfly the steaks and season both sides with salt and pepper. Spread the cream cheese across the cut side of each steak and evenly distribute the garlic over the cream cheese. Layer the mozzarella, Parmesan cheese, and spinach on top. Starting from the bottom of each steak, roll the meat upward tightly over the filling. Use about 6 toothpicks, evenly spaced, to secure the seam. Then slice in between the toothpicks, creating 1½- to 2-inch-thick rolls.
3. When the unit beeps to signify it has preheated, place the pinwheels on the Grill Grate, cut-side down. Close the hood and grill for 5 minutes.
4. After 5 minutes, open the hood and flip the pinwheels. Close the hood and cook for 5 minutes more.
5. When cooking is complete, check the meat for doneness. If you prefer your beef more well done, continue cooking to your liking. Remove the pinwheels from the grill and serve.
6. Cut the steak almost in half from one side (parallel to the cutting board), stopping just before you reach the other side. When you open the steak up, it'll be thinner and have two matching wings like a butterfly.

Swedish Beef Meatballs

Servings: 8 | Cooking Time: 12 Minutes

Ingredients:
- 1 pound ground beef
- 1 egg, beaten
- 2 carrots, shredded
- 2 bread slices, crumbled
- 1 small onion, minced
- ½ teaspoons garlic salt
- Pepper and salt, to taste
- 1 cup tomato sauce
- 2 cups pasta sauce

Directions:
1. Insert the Crisper Basket and close the hood. Select AIR CRISP, set the temperature to 400ºF, and set the time to 7 minutes. Select START/STOP to begin preheating.
2. In a bowl, combine the ground beef, egg, carrots, crumbled bread, onion, garlic salt, pepper and salt.
3. Divide the mixture into equal amounts and shape each one into a small meatball.
4. Put them in the Crisper Basket. Close the hood and AIR CRISP for 7 minutes.
5. Transfer the meatballs to an oven-safe dish and top with the tomato sauce and pasta sauce.
6. Set the dish into the pot and allow to AIR CRISP at 320ºF for 5 more minutes. Serve hot.

Lemongrass Beef Skewers

Servings: 4 | Cooking Time: 8 Minutes

Ingredients:
- 3 tablespoons minced garlic
- 3 tablespoons light brown sugar, packed
- 3 tablespoons lemongrass paste
- 1 tablespoon soy sauce
- 1 tablespoon peeled minced fresh ginger
- 1 tablespoon avocado oil
- ½ small red onion, minced
- 2 pounds sirloin steak, cut into 1-inch cubes
- Chopped fresh cilantro, for garnish

Directions:
1. In a large bowl, combine the garlic, brown sugar, lemongrass paste, soy sauce, ginger, avocado oil, and onion until the sugar is dissolved. Add the steak cubes and massage them with the marinade. Place 5 or 6 cubes on each of 6 to 8 skewers, then place the skewers in a large rimmed baking sheet and coat with the remaining marinade. Set aside to marinate for at least 30 minutes. If marinating for longer, cover and refrigerate.
2. Insert the Grill Grate and close the hood. Select GRILL, set the temperature to HI, and set the time to 8 minutes. Select START/STOP to begin preheating.
3. When the unit beeps to signify it has preheated, place the skewers on the Grill Grate. Close the hood and grill for 4 minutes.
4. After 4 minutes, open the hood and flip the skewers. Close the hood and cook for 4 minutes more. If you prefer extra char, add 2 minutes to the cook time.
5. When cooking is complete, remove the skewers from the grill and serve, garnished with the cilantro.

Honey-garlic Ribs

Servings: 6 | Cooking Time: 1 Hour 10 Minutes

Ingredients:
- 2 (2- to 3-pound) racks baby back ribs
- Sea salt
- ½ cup soy sauce
- 1 cup honey
- 4 garlic cloves, minced
- 1 teaspoon paprika
- 3 tablespoons light brown sugar, packed

Directions:
1. Insert the Grill Grate and close the hood. Select BAKE, set the temperature to 300°F, and set the time to 1 hour. Select START/STOP to begin preheating.
2. While the unit is preheating, generously season each rack with salt, then wrap each in aluminum foil.
3. When the unit beeps to signify it has preheated, place the foil-wrapped ribs on the Grill Grate. Close the hood and cook for 1 hour.
4. While the ribs are cooking, in a small bowl, combine the soy sauce, honey, garlic, paprika, and brown sugar until the sugar is dissolved.
5. When cooking is complete, remove the ribs from the grill. Slowly open the foil (but don't remove it) and brush the sauce over the ribs. Pour the remaining sauce over both racks.
6. Place the slightly opened packets of racks back onto the Grill Grate. Select GRILL, set the temperature to HI, and set the time to 10 minutes. Select START/STOP and then press the PREHEAT button to skip preheating. Close the hood and cook for 5 minutes.
7. After 5 minutes, open the hood, flip the rib racks, and place them back in the foil. Close the hood and cook for 5 minutes more or until you achieve your desired level of char.
8. When cooking is complete, remove the racks from the grill and serve.

Citrus Pork Loin Roast

Servings: 8 | Cooking Time: 45 Minutes

Ingredients:

- 1 tablespoon lime juice
- 1 tablespoon orange marmalade
- 1 teaspoon coarse brown mustard
- 1 teaspoon curry powder
- 1 teaspoon dried lemongrass
- 2 pound boneless pork loin roast
- Salt and ground black pepper, to taste
- Cooking spray

Directions:

1. Insert the Crisper Basket and close the hood. Select AIR CRISP, set the temperature to 360°F, and set the time to 45 minutes. Select START/STOP to begin preheating.
2. Mix the lime juice, marmalade, mustard, curry powder, and lemongrass.
3. Rub mixture all over the surface of the pork loin. Season with salt and pepper.
4. Spray the Crisper Basket with cooking spray and place pork roast diagonally in the basket.
5. Close the hood and AIR CRISP for 45 minutes, until the internal temperature reaches at least 145°F.
6. Wrap roast in foil and let rest for 10 minutes before slicing.
7. Serve immediately.

Crispy Pork Tenderloin

Servings: 6 | Cooking Time: 10 Minutes

Ingredients:

- 2 large egg whites
- 1½ tablespoons Dijon mustard
- 2 cups crushed pretzel crumbs
- 1½ pounds pork tenderloin, cut into ¼-pound sections
- Cooking spray

Directions:

1. Spritz the Crisper Basket with cooking spray.
2. Insert the Crisper Basket and close the hood. Select AIR CRISP, set the temperature to 350°F, and set the time to 10 minutes. Select START/STOP to begin preheating.
3. Whisk the egg whites with Dijon mustard in a bowl until bubbly. Pour the pretzel crumbs in a separate bowl.
4. Dredge the pork tenderloin in the egg white mixture and press to coat. Shake the excess off and roll the tenderloin over the pretzel crumbs.
5. Arrange the well-coated pork tenderloin in batches in a single layer in the Crisper Basket and spritz with cooking spray.
6. Close the hood and AIR CRISP for 10 minutes or until the pork is golden brown and crispy. Flip the pork halfway through. Repeat with remaining pork sections.
7. Serve immediately.

Crackling Pork Roast

Servings: 8 | Cooking Time: 1 Hour 30 Minutes

Ingredients:

- 1 (3- to 4-pound) boneless pork shoulder, rind on
- Kosher salt

Directions:

1. Pat the roast dry with a paper towel. Using a sharp knife, score the rind, creating a diamond pattern on top. Season generously with salt. Place it in the refrigerator, uncovered, overnight to brine.
2. Plug the thermometer into the unit. Insert the Cooking Pot and close the hood. Select ROAST, set the temperature to 350°F, then select PRESET. Use the arrows to the right to select PORK. The unit will default to WELL to cook pork to a safe temperature. Insert the Smart Thermometer into the thickest part of the meat. Select START/STOP to begin preheating.
3. When the unit beeps to signify it has preheated, place the roast in the Cooking Pot. Close the hood to begin cooking.
4. When cooking is complete, the Smart Thermometer will indicate that the desired temperature has been reached. Remove the pork and let it rest for 10 minutes before slicing.

Smoked Beef

Servings: 8 | Cooking Time: 45 Minutes

Ingredients:
- 2 pounds roast beef, at room temperature
- 2 tablespoons extra-virgin olive oil
- 1 teaspoon sea salt flakes
- 1 teaspoon ground black pepper
- 1 teaspoon smoked paprika
- Few dashes of liquid smoke
- 2 jalapeño peppers, thinly sliced

Directions:
1. Select ROAST, set the temperature to 330ºF, and set the time to 45 minutes. Select START/STOP to begin preheating.
2. With kitchen towels, pat the beef dry.
3. Massage the extra-virgin olive oil, salt, black pepper, and paprika into the meat. Cover with liquid smoke.
4. Put the beef in the pot. Close the hood and ROAST for 30 minutes. Flip the roast over and allow to roast for another 15 minutes.
5. When cooked through, serve topped with sliced jalapeños.

Korean-style Steak Tips

Servings: 4 | Cooking Time: 13 Minutes

Ingredients:
- 4 garlic cloves, minced
- ½ apple, peeled and grated
- 3 tablespoons sesame oil
- 3 tablespoons brown sugar
- $\frac{1}{3}$ cup soy sauce
- 1 teaspoon freshly ground black pepper
- Sea salt
- 1½ pounds beef tips

Directions:
1. In a medium bowl, combine the garlic, apple, sesame oil, sugar, soy sauce, pepper, and salt until well mixed.
2. Place the beef tips in a large shallow bowl and pour the marinade over them. Cover and refrigerate for 30 minutes.
3. Insert the Grill Grate and close the hood. Select GRILL, set the temperature to MEDIUM, and set the time to 13 minutes. Select START/STOP to begin preheating.
4. When the unit beeps to signify it has preheated, place the steak tips on the Grill Grate. Close the hood and GRILL for 11 minutes.
5. Cooking is complete to medium doneness when the internal temperature of the meat reaches 145ºF on a food thermometer. If desired, GRILL for up to 2 minutes more.
6. Remove the steak, and set it on a cutting board to rest for 5 minutes. Serve.

Brown-sugared Ham

Servings: 6 To 8 | Cooking Time: 30 Minutes

Ingredients:
- 1 (3-pound) bone-in, fully cooked ham quarter
- 3 tablespoons Dijon mustard
- ¼ cup pineapple juice
- ¼ cup apple cider vinegar
- 1 cup light brown sugar, packed
- 1 teaspoon cinnamon
- ½ teaspoon ground ginger

Directions:
1. Plug the thermometer into the unit. Insert the Cooking Pot and close the hood. Select ROAST, set the temperature to 350°F, then select PRESET. Use the arrows to the right to select PORK. The unit will default to WELL to cook pork to a safe temperature. Insert the Smart Thermometer into the thickest part of the ham. Select START/STOP to begin preheating.
2. While the unit is preheating, score the ham using a sharp knife, creating a diamond pattern on top. Brush on the Dijon mustard.
3. In a small bowl, combine the pineapple juice, vinegar, brown sugar, cinnamon, and ginger.
4. When the unit beeps to signify it has preheated, place the ham in the Cooking Pot. Brush some of the glaze over the entire ham, then pour the rest on top so the glaze can seep into the scores. Close the hood to begin cooking.
5. When cooking is complete, the Smart Thermometer will indicate that the desired temperature has been reached. Remove the ham from the pot and let rest for at least 10 minutes before slicing. Serve.

Homemade Teriyaki Pork Ribs

Servings: 4 | Cooking Time: 30 Minutes

Ingredients:
- ¼ cup soy sauce
- ¼ cup honey
- 1 teaspoon garlic powder
- 1 teaspoon ground dried ginger
- 4 boneless country-style pork ribs
- Cooking spray

Directions:
1. Spritz the Crisper Basket with cooking spray.
2. Insert the Crisper Basket and close the hood. Select AIR CRISP, set the temperature to 350ºF, and set the time to 30 minutes. Select START/STOP to begin preheating.
3. Make the teriyaki sauce: combine the soy sauce, honey, garlic powder, and ginger in a bowl. Stir to mix well.
4. Brush the ribs with half of the teriyaki sauce, then arrange the ribs in the basket. Spritz with cooking spray. You may need to work in batches to avoid overcrowding.
5. Close the hood and AIR CRISP for 30 minutes or until the internal temperature of the ribs reaches at least 145ºF. Brush the ribs with remaining teriyaki sauce and flip halfway through.
6. Serve immediately.

Miso Marinated Steak

Servings: 4 | Cooking Time: 12 Minutes

Ingredients:
- ¾ pound flank steak
- 1½ tablespoons sake
- 1 tablespoon brown miso paste
- 1 teaspoon honey
- 2 cloves garlic, pressed
- 1 tablespoon olive oil

Directions:
1. Put all the ingredients in a Ziploc bag. Shake to cover the steak well with the seasonings and refrigerate for at least 1 hour.
2. Insert the Crisper Basket and close the hood. Select AIR CRISP, set the temperature to 400ºF, and set the time to 12 minutes. Select START/STOP to begin preheating.
3. Coat all sides of the steak with cooking spray. Put the steak in the basket.
4. Close the hood and AIR CRISP for 12 minutes, turning the steak twice during the cooking time, then serve immediately.

Crispy Pork Belly Bites

Servings: 6 | Cooking Time: 20 Minutes

Ingredients:
- 1 tablespoon garlic powder
- 1 tablespoon sea salt
- 1 tablespoon paprika
- ¼ teaspoon freshly ground black pepper
- 2 pounds pork belly (3 to 4 slabs)

Directions:
1. Insert the Grill Grate and close the hood. Select GRILL, set the temperature to HI, and set the time to 20 minutes. Select START/STOP to begin preheating.
2. While the unit is preheating, in a large bowl, combine the garlic powder, salt, paprika, and pepper.
3. Pat the pork belly dry with a paper towel. Place it in the seasoning and toss to generously coat the pork belly on all sides.
4. When the unit beeps to signify it has preheated, place the pork belly on the Grill Grate, skin-side up. Close the hood and grill for 10 minutes.
5. After 10 minutes, open the hood and flip the pork. Close the hood and cook for 10 minutes more.
6. When cooking is complete, remove the pork belly from the grill and serve.

Cheesy Jalapeño Popper Burgers

Servings: 4 | Cooking Time: 9 Minutes

Ingredients:
- 2 jalapeño peppers, seeded, stemmed, and minced
- ½ cup shredded Cheddar cheese
- 4 ounces cream cheese, at room temperature
- 4 slices bacon, cooked and crumbled
- 2 pounds ground beef
- ½ teaspoon chili powder
- ¼ teaspoon paprika
- ¼ teaspoon freshly ground black pepper
- 4 hamburger buns
- 4 slices pepper Jack cheese
- Lettuce, sliced tomato, and sliced red onion, for topping (optional)

Directions:
1. Insert the Grill Grate and close the hood. Select GRILL, set the temperature to HIGH, and set the time to 9 minutes. Select START/STOP to begin preheating.
2. In a medium bowl, combine the peppers, Cheddar cheese, cream cheese, and bacon until well combined.
3. Form the ground beef into 8¼-inch-thick patties. Spoon some of the filling mixture onto four of the patties, then place a second patty on top of each to make four burgers. Use your fingers to pinch the edges of the patties together to seal in the filling. Reshape the patties with your hands as needed.
4. Combine the chili powder, paprika, and pepper in a small bowl. Sprinkle the mixture onto both sides of the burgers.
5. When the units beeps to signify it has preheated, place the burgers on the Grill Grate. Close the hood and GRILL for 4 minutes without flipping. Cooking is complete when the internal temperature of the beef reaches at least 145ºF on a food thermometer. If needed, GRILL for up to 5 more minutes.
6. Place the burgers on the hamburger buns and top with pepper Jack cheese. Add lettuce, tomato, and red onion, if desired.

Steak And Lettuce Salad

Servings: 4 To 6 | Cooking Time: 16 Minutes

Ingredients:

- 4 skirt steaks
- Sea salt, to taste
- Freshly ground black pepper, to taste
- 6 cups chopped romaine lettuce
- ¾ cup cherry tomatoes, halved
- ¼ cup blue cheese, crumbled
- 1 cup croutons
- 2 avocados, peeled and sliced
- 1 cup blue cheese dressing

Directions:

1. Insert the Grill Grate and close the hood. Select GRILL, set the temperature to HIGH, and set the time to 8 minutes. Select START/STOP to begin preheating.
2. Season the steaks on both sides with the salt and pepper.
3. When the unit beeps to signify it has preheated, place 2 steaks on the Grill Grate. Gently press the steaks down to maximize grill marks. Close the hood and GRILL for 4 minutes. After 4 minutes, flip the steaks, close the hood, and GRILL for an additional 4 minutes.
4. Remove the steaks from the grill and transfer to them a cutting board. Tent with aluminum foil.
5. Repeat step 3 with the remaining 2 steaks.
6. While the second set of steaks is cooking, assemble the salad by tossing together the lettuce, tomatoes, blue cheese crumbles, and croutons. Top with the avocado slices.
7. Once the second set of steaks has finished cooking, slice all four of the steaks into thin strips, and place on top of the salad. Drizzle with the blue cheese dressing and serve.

Garlic Herb Crusted Lamb

Servings: 6 | Cooking Time: 1 Hour

Ingredients:

- ¼ cup red wine vinegar
- 3 garlic cloves, minced
- 1 tablespoon garlic powder
- 1 tablespoon paprika
- 1 tablespoon ground cumin
- 1 tablespoon dried parsley
- 1 tablespoon dried thyme
- 1 tablespoon dried oregano
- 1 teaspoon salt
- ½ teaspoon freshly ground black pepper
- Juice of ½ lemon
- 1 (3-pound) boneless leg of lamb

Directions:

1. In a large bowl, mix together the vinegar, garlic, garlic powder, paprika, cumin, parsley, thyme, oregano, salt, pepper, and lemon juice until well combined—the marinade will turn into a thick paste. Add the leg of lamb and massage the marinade into the meat. Coat the lamb with the marinade and let sit for at least 30 minutes. If marinating for longer, cover and refrigerate.
2. Plug the thermometer into the unit. Insert the Grill Grate and close the hood. Select GRILL, set the temperature to LO, and set the time to 30 minutes. Insert the Smart Thermometer into the thickest part of the meat. Select START/STOP to begin preheating.
3. When the unit beeps to signify it has preheated, place the lamb on the Grill Grate. Select the BEEF/LAMB preset and choose MEDIUM-WELL or according to your desired doneness. Close the hood and cook for 30 minutes.
4. After 30 minutes, which is the maximum time for the LO setting, select GRILL again, set the temperature to LO, and set the time to 30 minutes. Select START/STOP and press PREHEAT to skip preheating. Cook until the Smart Thermometer indicates that the desired internal temperature has been reached.
5. When cooking is complete, remove the lamb from the grill and serve.

Pork Chops With Creamy Mushroom Sauce

Servings: 6 | Cooking Time: 10 Minutes

Ingredients:
- 1 cup heavy (whipping) cream
- ½ cup chicken broth
- 1 tablespoon cornstarch
- 1 teaspoon garlic powder
- 6 (6-ounce) boneless pork chops
- 8 ounces mushrooms, sliced

Directions:
1. Insert the Grill Grate and close the hood. Select GRILL, set the temperature to HI, and set the time to 10 minutes. Select START/STOP to begin preheating.
2. While the unit is preheating, in a medium bowl, whisk together the heavy cream, chicken broth, cornstarch, and garlic powder.
3. When the unit beeps to signify it has preheated, place the pork chops on the Grill Grate. Close the hood and grill for 5 minutes.
4. After 5 minutes, open the hood and use grill mitts to remove the Grill Grate and the chops. Pour the cream mixture into the Cooking Pot. Put the Grill Grate back into the unit and flip the pork chops. Close the hood and cook for 5 minutes more.
5. When cooking is complete, remove the pork chops from the grill. Use grill mitts to remove the Grill Grate from the unit and stir the cream mixture. Add the sliced mushrooms, close the hood, and let sit for 5 minutes. Pour the creamy mushroom sauce over the pork chops and serve.

Simple Pork Meatballs With Red Chili

Servings: 4 | Cooking Time: 15 Minutes

Ingredients:
- 1 pound ground pork
- 2 cloves garlic, finely minced
- 1 cup scallions, finely chopped
- 1½ tablespoons Worcestershire sauce
- ½ teaspoon freshly grated ginger root
- 1 teaspoon turmeric powder
- 1 tablespoon oyster sauce
- 1 small sliced red chili, for garnish
- Cooking spray

Directions:
1. Spritz the Crisper Basket with cooking spray.
2. Insert the Crisper Basket and close the hood. Select AIR CRISP, set the temperature to 350°F, and set the time to 15 minutes. Select START/STOP to begin preheating.
3. Combine all the ingredients, except for the red chili in a large bowl. Toss to mix well.
4. Shape the mixture into equally sized balls, then arrange them in the basket and spritz with cooking spray.
5. Close the hood and AIR CRISP for 15 minutes or until the balls are lightly browned. Flip the balls halfway through.
6. Serve the pork meatballs with red chili on top.

Classic Walliser Schnitzel

Servings: 2 | Cooking Time: 14 Minutes

Ingredients:
- ½ cup pork rinds
- ½ tablespoon fresh parsley
- ½ teaspoon fennel seed
- ½ teaspoon mustard
- ⅓ tablespoon cider vinegar
- 1 teaspoon garlic salt
- ⅓ teaspoon ground black pepper
- 2 eggs
- 2 pork schnitzel, halved
- Cooking spray

Directions:
1. Spritz the Crisper Basket with cooking spray.
2. Insert the Crisper Basket and close the hood. Select AIR CRISP, set the temperature to 350ºF, and set the time to 14 minutes. Select START/STOP to begin preheating.
3. Put the pork rinds, parsley, fennel seeds, and mustard in a food processor. Pour in the vinegar and sprinkle with salt and ground black pepper. Pulse until well combined and smooth.
4. Pour the pork rind mixture in a large bowl. Whisk the eggs in a separate bowl.
5. Dunk the pork schnitzel in the whisked eggs, then dunk in the pork rind mixture to coat well. Shake the excess off.
6. Arrange the schnitzel in the basket and spritz with cooking spray. Close the hood and AIR CRISP for 14 minutes or until golden and crispy. Flip the schnitzel halfway through.
7. Serve immediately.

Grilled Kalbi Beef Short Ribs

Servings: 4 | Cooking Time: 10 Minutes

Ingredients:
- ½ cup soy sauce
- ¼ cup water
- ½ cup light brown sugar, packed
- ¼ cup honey
- 2 tablespoons sesame oil
- ½ teaspoon onion powder
- 1 teaspoon garlic powder
- 1 teaspoon peeled minced fresh ginger
- 3 pounds short ribs
- 1 scallion, both white and green parts, sliced, for garnish
- Sesame seeds, for garnish

Directions:
1. In a large bowl, combine the soy sauce, water, brown sugar, honey, sesame oil, onion powder, garlic powder, and minced ginger until the sugar is dissolved. Place the short ribs in the bowl and massage the marinade into the meat. Set aside to marinate for at least 30 minutes. If marinating for longer, cover and refrigerate.
2. Insert the Grill Grate and close the hood. Select GRILL, set the temperature to HI, and set the time to 10 minutes. Select START/STOP to begin preheating.
3. When the unit beeps to signify it has preheated, place the short ribs on the Grill Grate. Close the hood and cook for 5 minutes.
4. After 5 minutes, open the hood and flip the short ribs. Close the hood and cook for 5 minutes more.
5. When cooking is complete, remove the short ribs from the grill and garnish with the scallions and sesame seeds. Serve.

Pork Spareribs With Peanut Sauce

Servings: 6 | Cooking Time: 30 Minutes

Ingredients:
- 2 (2- to 3-pound) racks St. Louis–style spareribs
- Sea salt
- ½ cup crunchy peanut butter
- 1 tablespoon rice vinegar
- 2 tablespoons hoisin sauce
- 1 tablespoon honey
- 2 tablespoons soy sauce
- 1 teaspoon garlic powder

Directions:
1. Plug the thermometer into the unit. Insert the Grill Grate and close the hood. Select GRILL, set the temperature to MED, and select PRESET. Use the arrows to the right to select PORK. The unit will default to WELL to cook the pork to a safe temperature. Insert the Smart Thermometer into the thickest part of the meat between two bones, making sure it does not touch bone. Select START/STOP to begin preheating.
2. When the unit beeps to signify it has preheated, place the racks of ribs on the Grill Grate. Close the hood to begin cooking.
3. When the Foodi™ Grill indicates it's time to flip, open the hood and flip the racks. Then close the hood to continue cooking.
4. While the ribs are cooking, in a small bowl, combine the peanut butter, vinegar, hoisin sauce, honey, soy sauce, and garlic powder and mix until well blended.
5. When cooking is complete, the Smart Thermometer will indicate that the desired internal temperature has been reached. Open the hood and remove the ribs. Either pour the sauce over the ribs or divide the sauce between individual bowls for dipping. Serve.

Apple-glazed Pork

Servings: 4 | Cooking Time: 19 Minutes

Ingredients:
- 1 sliced apple
- 1 small onion, sliced
- 2 tablespoons apple cider vinegar, divided
- ½ teaspoon thyme
- ½ teaspoon rosemary
- ¼ teaspoon brown sugar
- 3 tablespoons olive oil, divided
- ¼ teaspoon smoked paprika
- 4 pork chops
- Salt and ground black pepper, to taste

Directions:
1. Select BAKE, set the temperature to 350ºF, and set the time to 4 minutes. Select START/STOP to begin preheating.
2. Combine the apple slices, onion, 1 tablespoon of vinegar, thyme, rosemary, brown sugar, and 2 tablespoons of olive oil in a baking pan. Stir to mix well.
3. Place the pan directly in the pot. Close the hood and BAKE for 4 minutes.
4. Meanwhile, combine the remaining vinegar and olive oil, and paprika in a large bowl. Sprinkle with salt and ground black pepper. Stir to mix well. Dredge the pork in the mixture and toss to coat well.
5. Remove the baking pan from the grill and put in the pork. Place the pan directly in the pot. Close the hood and AIR CRISP for 10 minutes to lightly brown the pork. Flip the pork chops halfway through.
6. Remove the pork from the grill and baste with baked apple mixture on both sides. Put the pork back to the grill and AIR CRISP for an additional 5 minutes. Flip halfway through.
7. Serve immediately.

POULTRY

POULTRY

Deep Fried Duck Leg Quarters

Servings: 4 | Cooking Time: 45 Minutes

Ingredients:
- 4 skin-on duck leg quarters
- 2 medium garlic cloves, minced
- ½ teaspoon salt
- ½ teaspoon ground black pepper

Directions:
1. Spritz the Crisper Basket with cooking spray.
2. Insert the Crisper Basket and close the hood. Select AIR CRISP, set the temperature to 300ºF, and set the time to 45 minutes. Select START/STOP to begin preheating.
3. On a clean work surface, rub the duck leg quarters with garlic, salt, and black pepper.
4. Arrange the leg quarters in the basket and spritz with cooking spray.
5. Close the hood and AIR CRISP for 30 minutes, then flip the leg quarters and increase the temperature to 375ºF. AIR CRISP for 15 more minutes or until well browned and crispy.
6. Remove the duck leg quarters from the grill and allow to cool for 10 minutes before serving.

Orange And Honey Glazed Duck With Apples

Servings: 2 To 3 | Cooking Time: 15 Minutes

Ingredients:
- 1 pound duck breasts
- Kosher salt and pepper, to taste
- Juice and zest of 1 orange
- ¼ cup honey
- 2 sprigs thyme, plus more for garnish
- 2 firm tart apples, such as Fuji

Directions:
1. Insert the Crisper Basket and close the hood. Select ROAST, set the temperature to 400ºF, and set the time to 13 minutes. Select START/STOP to begin preheating.
2. Pat the duck breasts dry and, using a sharp knife, make 3 to 4 shallow, diagonal slashes in the skin. Turn the breasts and score the skin on the diagonal in the opposite direction to create a cross-hatch pattern. Season well with salt and pepper.
3. Place the duck breasts skin-side up in the Crisper Basket. Close the hood and ROAST for 8 minutes. Flip and roast for 4 more minutes on the second side.
4. While the duck is roasting, prepare the sauce. Combine the orange juice and zest, honey, and thyme in a small saucepan. Bring to a boil, stirring to dissolve the honey, then reduce the heat and simmer until thickened. Core the apples and cut into quarters. Cut each quarter into 3 or 4 slices depending on the size.
5. After the duck has cooked on both sides, turn it and brush the skin with the orange-honey glaze. Roast for 1 more minute. Remove the duck breasts to a cutting board and allow to rest.
6. Toss the apple slices with the remaining orange-honey sauce in a medium bowl. Arrange the apples in a single layer in the Crisper Basket. AIR CRISP for 10 minutes while the duck breast rests. Slice the duck breasts on the bias and divide them and the apples among 2 or 3 plates.
7. Serve warm, garnished with additional thyme.

Easy Asian Turkey Meatballs

Servings: 4 | Cooking Time: 11 To 14 Minutes

Ingredients:
- 2 tablespoons peanut oil, divided
- 1 small onion, minced
- ¼ cup water chestnuts, finely chopped
- ½ teaspoon ground ginger
- 2 tablespoons low-sodium soy sauce
- ¼ cup panko bread crumbs
- 1 egg, beaten
- 1 pound ground turkey

Directions:
1. Select AIR CRISP, set the temperature to 400ºF, and set the time to 2 minutes. Select START/STOP to begin preheating.
2. In a round metal pan, combine 1 tablespoon of peanut oil and onion. Place the pan directly in the pot. Close the hood and AIR CRISP for 1 to 2 minutes or until crisp and tender. Transfer the onion to a medium bowl.
3. Add the water chestnuts, ground ginger, soy sauce, and bread crumbs to the onion and mix well. Add egg and stir well. Mix in the ground turkey until combined.
4. Form the mixture into 1-inch meatballs. Drizzle the remaining 1 tablespoon of oil over the meatballs. Arrange the meatballs in the pan.
5. Place the pan directly in the pot. Close the hood and BAKE for 10 to 12 minutes, or until they are 165ºF on a meat thermometer. Rest for 5 minutes before serving.

Potato Cheese Crusted Chicken

Servings: 4 | Cooking Time: 22 To 25 Minutes

Ingredients:
- ¼ cup buttermilk
- 1 large egg, beaten
- 1 cup instant potato flakes
- ¼ cup grated Parmesan cheese
- 1 teaspoon salt
- ½ teaspoon freshly ground black pepper
- 2 whole boneless, skinless chicken breasts, halved
- Cooking spray

Directions:
1. Insert the Crisper Basket and close the hood. Select BAKE, set the temperature to 325ºF, and set the time to 25 minutes. Select START/STOP to begin preheating.
2. Line the Crisper Basket with parchment paper.
3. In a shallow bowl, whisk the buttermilk and egg until blended. In another shallow bowl, stir together the potato flakes, cheese, salt, and pepper.
4. One at a time, dip the chicken pieces in the buttermilk mixture and the potato flake mixture, coating thoroughly.
5. Place the coated chicken on the parchment and spritz with cooking spray.
6. Close the hood and BAKE for 15 minutes. Flip the chicken, spritz it with cooking spray, and bake for 7 to 10 minutes more until the outside is crispy and the inside is no longer pink. Serve immediately.

Adobo Chicken

Servings: 4 | Cooking Time: 15 Minutes

Ingredients:
- 2 tablespoons soy sauce
- 2 tablespoons rice vinegar
- 1 tablespoon balsamic vinegar
- ¼ teaspoon freshly ground black pepper
- 4 garlic cloves, minced
- ½ teaspoon peeled minced fresh ginger
- Juice of ½ lemon
- ¼ teaspoon granulated sugar
- 3 bay leaves
- Pinch Italian seasoning (optional)
- Pinch ground cumin (optional)
- 3 pounds chicken drumsticks

Directions:
1. In a large bowl, whisk together the soy sauce, rice vinegar, balsamic vinegar, pepper, garlic, ginger, lemon juice, sugar, bay leaves, Italian seasoning (if using), and cumin (if using). Add the drumsticks to the marinade, making sure the meat is coated. Cover and refrigerate for at least 1 hour. If you have the time, marinate the chicken overnight to let all the flavors settle in.
2. Insert the Grill Grate and close the hood. Select GRILL, set the temperature to MED, and set the time to 15 minutes. Select START/STOP to begin preheating.
3. When the unit beeps to signify it has preheated, place the chicken drumsticks on the Grill Grate. Brush any leftover marinade onto the drumsticks. Close the hood and grill for 8 minutes.
4. After 8 minutes, open the hood and flip the drumsticks. Close the hood and continue cooking for 7 minutes more.
5. When cooking is complete, remove the drumsticks from the grill and serve.

Cilantro-lime Chicken Thighs

Servings: 4 | Cooking Time: 15 Minutes

Ingredients:
- ½ cup extra-virgin olive oil
- 4 tablespoons light brown sugar, packed
- 4 tablespoons soy sauce
- Juice of 2 key limes
- Zest of 1 key lime
- 2 teaspoons sea salt
- ½ teaspoon freshly ground black pepper
- 2 tablespoons minced garlic
- ½ cup chopped fresh cilantro
- 3 pounds bone-in, skin-on chicken thighs

Directions:
1. In a large bowl, whisk together the olive oil, brown sugar, soy sauce, lime juice, lime zest, salt, pepper, minced garlic, and cilantro. Place the chicken thighs in the marinade and turn so the meat is fully coated. Cover the bowl and refrigerate for at least 1 hour or up to overnight.
2. Insert the Grill Grate and close the hood. Select GRILL, set the temperature to LO, and set the time to 15 minutes. Select START/STOP to begin preheating.
3. When the unit beeps to signify it has preheated, place the chicken thighs skin-side up on the Grill Grate. Brush some of the marinade on the chicken. Close the hood and grill for 8 minutes.
4. After 8 minutes, open the hood and flip the chicken. Close the hood and continue cooking for 7 minutes more.

Spicy Chicken Kebabs

Servings: 4 | Cooking Time: 14 Minutes

Ingredients:

- 1 tablespoon ground cumin
- 1 tablespoon garlic powder
- 1 tablespoon chili powder
- 2 teaspoons paprika
- ¼ teaspoon sea salt
- ¼ teaspoon freshly ground black pepper
- 1 pound boneless, skinless chicken breasts, cut in

2-inch cubes
- 2 tablespoons extra-virgin olive oil, divided
- 2 red bell peppers, seeded and cut into 1-inch cubes
- 1 red onion, quartered
- Juice of 1 lime

Directions:

1. In a small mixing bowl, combine the cumin, garlic powder, chili powder, paprika, salt, and pepper, and mix well.
2. Place the chicken, 1 tablespoon oil, and half of the spice mixture into a large resealable plastic bag or container. Toss to coat evenly.
3. Place the bell pepper, onion, remaining 1 tablespoon of oil, and remaining spice mixture into a large resealable plastic bag or container. Toss to coat evenly. Refrigerate the chicken and vegetables for at least 30 minutes.
4. Insert the Grill Grate and close the hood. Select GRILL, set the temperature to HIGH, and set the time to 14 minutes. Select START/STOP to begin preheating.
5. While the unit is preheating, assemble the kebabs by threading the chicken onto the wood skewers, alternating with the peppers and onion. Ensure the ingredients are pushed almost completely down to the end of the skewers.
6. When the unit beeps to signify it has preheated, place the skewers on the Grill Grate. Close the hood and GRILL for 10 to 14 minutes.
7. Cooking is complete when the internal temperature of the chicken reaches 165ºF. When cooking is complete, remove from the heat, and drizzle with lime juice.

Lemony Chicken And Veggie Kebabs

Servings: 4 | Cooking Time: 14 Minutes

Ingredients:

- 2 tablespoons plain Greek yogurt
- ¼ cup extra-virgin olive oil
- Juice of 4 lemons
- Grated zest of 1 lemon
- 4 garlic cloves, minced
- 2 tablespoons dried oregano
- 1 teaspoon sea salt
- ½ teaspoon freshly ground black pepper
- 1 pound boneless, skinless chicken breasts, cut into 2-inch cubes
- 1 red onion, quartered
- 1 zucchini, sliced

Directions:

1. In a large bowl, whisk together the Greek yogurt, oil, lemon juice, zest, garlic, oregano, salt, and pepper until well combined.
2. Place the chicken and half of the marinade into a large resealable plastic bag or container. Move the chicken around to coat evenly. Refrigerate for at least 30 minutes.
3. Insert the Grill Grate and close the hood. Select GRILL, set the temperature to MEDIUM, and set the time to 14 minutes. Select START/STOP to begin preheating.
4. While the unit is preheating, assemble the kebabs by threading the chicken on the wood skewers, alternating with the red onion and zucchini. Ensure the ingredients are pushed almost completely down to the end of the skewers.
5. When the unit beeps to signify it has preheated, place the skewers on the Grill Grate. Close hood and GRILL for 10 to 14 minutes, occasionally basting the kebabs with the remaining marinade while cooking.
6. Cooking is complete when the internal temperature of the chicken reaches 165ºF on a food thermometer.

Lime Chicken With Cilantro

Servings: 4 | Cooking Time: 20 Minutes

Ingredients:
- 4 boneless, skinless chicken breasts
- ½ cup chopped fresh cilantro
- Juice of 1 lime
- Chicken seasoning or rub, to taste
- Salt and ground black pepper, to taste
- Cooking spray

Directions:
1. Put the chicken breasts in the large bowl, then add the cilantro, lime juice, chicken seasoning, salt, and black pepper. Toss to coat well.
2. Wrap the bowl in plastic and refrigerate to marinate for at least 30 minutes.
3. Spritz the Crisper Basket with cooking spray.
4. Insert the Crisper Basket and close the hood. Select AIR CRISP, set the temperature to 400°F, and set the time to 10 minutes. Select START/STOP to begin preheating.
5. Remove the marinated chicken breasts from the bowl and place in the preheated grill. Spritz with cooking spray. You may need to work in batches to avoid overcrowding.
6. Close the hood and AIR CRISP for 10 minutes or until the internal temperature of the chicken reaches at least 165°F. Flip the breasts halfway through.
7. Serve immediately.

Rosemary Turkey Breast

Servings: 6 | Cooking Time: 30 Minutes

Ingredients:
- ½ teaspoon dried rosemary
- 2 minced garlic cloves
- 2 teaspoons salt
- 1 teaspoon ground black pepper
- ¼ cup olive oil
- 2½ pounds turkey breast
- ¼ cup pure maple syrup
- 1 tablespoon stone-ground brown mustard
- 1 tablespoon melted vegan butter

Directions:
1. Combine the rosemary, garlic, salt, ground black pepper, and olive oil in a large bowl. Stir to mix well.
2. Dunk the turkey breast in the mixture and wrap the bowl in plastic. Refrigerate for 2 hours to marinate.
3. Remove the bowl from the refrigerator and let sit for half an hour before cooking.
4. Spritz the Crisper Basket with cooking spray.
5. Insert the Crisper Basket and close the hood. Select AIR CRISP, set the temperature to 400°F, and set the time to 30 minutes. Select START/STOP to begin preheating.
6. Remove the turkey from the marinade and place in the basket. Close the hood and AIR CRISP for 20 minutes or until well browned. Flip the breast halfway through.
7. Meanwhile, combine the remaining ingredients in a small bowl. Stir to mix well.
8. Pour half of the butter mixture over the turkey breast in the basket. Close the hood and AIR CRISP for 10 more minutes. Flip the breast and pour the remaining half of butter mixture over halfway through.
9. Transfer the turkey on a plate and slice to serve.

Fried Buffalo Chicken Taquitos

Servings: 6 | Cooking Time: 5 To 10 Minutes

Ingredients:
- 8 ounces fat-free cream cheese, softened
- ⅛ cup Buffalo sauce
- 2 cups shredded cooked chicken
- 12 low-carb flour tortillas
- Olive oil spray

Directions:
1. Spray the Crisper Basket lightly with olive oil spray.
2. Insert the Crisper Basket and close the hood. Select AIR CRISP, set the temperature to 360ºF, and set the time to 10 minutes. Select START/STOP to begin preheating.
3. In a large bowl, mix together the cream cheese and Buffalo sauce until well combined. Add the chicken and stir until combined.
4. Place the tortillas on a clean workspace. Spoon 2 to 3 tablespoons of the chicken mixture in a thin line down the center of each tortilla. Roll up the tortillas.
5. Place the tortillas in the Crisper Basket, seam-side down. Spray each tortilla lightly with olive oil spray. You may need to cook the taquitos in batches.
6. Close the hood and AIR CRISP for 5 to 10 minutes until golden brown.
7. Serve hot.

Soy-garlic Crispy Chicken

Servings: 4 | Cooking Time: 20 Minutes

Ingredients:
- 20 to 24 chicken wings
- 2 tablespoons cornstarch
- ¼ cup soy sauce
- ½ cup water
- 1 tablespoon sesame oil
- 1 teaspoon peeled minced fresh ginger
- 1 teaspoon garlic powder
- 1 teaspoon onion powder
- 1 tablespoon oyster sauce
- 2 tablespoons honey
- 1 tablespoon rice vinegar
- 1 tablespoon light brown sugar, packed

Directions:
1. Insert the Grill Grate and close the hood. Select GRILL, set the temperature to MED, and set the time to 20 minutes. Select START/STOP to begin preheating.
2. While the unit is preheating, pat the chicken wings dry with a paper towel and place them in a large bowl. Sprinkle the wings with the cornstarch and toss to coat.
3. In a separate large bowl, whisk together the soy sauce, water, sesame oil, ginger, garlic powder, onion powder, oyster sauce, honey, rice vinegar, and brown sugar until the sugar is dissolved. Place half the sauce in a small bowl and set aside.
4. When the unit beeps to signify it has preheated, place the chicken wings on the Grill Grate. Close the hood and cook for 10 minutes.
5. After 10 minutes, open the hood and flip the wings. Using a basting brush, brush the soy-garlic sauce from the small bowl on the chicken wings. Close the hood and cook for 10 minutes more.
6. When cooking is complete, remove the wings from the grill and place in the large bowl with the remaining soy-garlic sauce. Toss and coat the wings with the sauce, then serve.

Sweet-and-sour Drumsticks

Servings: 4 | Cooking Time: 23 To 25 Minutes

Ingredients:
- 6 chicken drumsticks
- 3 tablespoons lemon juice, divided
- 3 tablespoons low-sodium soy sauce, divided
- 1 tablespoon peanut oil
- 3 tablespoons honey
- 3 tablespoons brown sugar
- 2 tablespoons ketchup
- ¼ cup pineapple juice

Directions:
1. Insert the Crisper Basket and close the hood. Select BAKE, set the temperature to 350°F, and set the time to 18 minutes. Select START/STOP to begin preheating.
2. Sprinkle the drumsticks with 1 tablespoon of lemon juice and 1 tablespoon of soy sauce. Place in the Crisper Basket and drizzle with the peanut oil. Toss to coat. Close the hood and BAKE for 18 minutes, or until the chicken is almost done.
3. Meanwhile, in a metal bowl, combine the remaining 2 tablespoons of lemon juice, the remaining 2 tablespoons of soy sauce, honey, brown sugar, ketchup, and pineapple juice.
4. Add the cooked chicken to the bowl and stir to coat the chicken well with the sauce.
5. Place the metal bowl in the basket. Bake for 5 to 7 minutes or until the chicken is glazed and registers 165°F on a meat thermometer. Serve warm.

Fried Chicken Piccata

Servings: 2 | Cooking Time: 22 Minutes

Ingredients:
- 2 large eggs
- ½ cup all-purpose flour
- ½ teaspoon freshly ground black pepper
- 2 boneless, skinless chicken breasts
- 4 tablespoons unsalted butter
- Juice of 1 lemon
- 1 tablespoon capers, drained

Directions:
1. Insert the Crisper Basket and close the hood. Select AIR CRISP, set the temperature to 375°F, and set the time to 22 minutes. Select START/STOP to begin preheating.
2. Meanwhile, in a medium shallow bowl, whisk the eggs until they are fully beaten.
3. In a separate medium shallow bowl, combine the flour and black pepper, using a fork to distribute the pepper evenly throughout.
4. Dredge the chicken in the flour to coat it completely, then dip it into the egg, then back in the flour.
5. When the unit beeps to signify it has preheated, place the chicken in the basket. Close the hood and AIR CRISP for 18 minutes.
6. While the chicken is cooking, melt the butter in a skillet over medium heat. Add the lemon juice and capers, and bring to a simmer. Reduce the heat to low, and simmer for 4 minutes.
7. After 18 minutes, check the chicken. Cooking is complete when the internal temperature of the meat reaches at least 165°F on a food thermometer. If necessary, close the hood and continue cooking for up to 3 minutes more.
8. Plate the chicken, and drizzle the butter sauce over each serving.

Blackened Chicken

Servings: 4 | Cooking Time: 10 Minutes

Ingredients:
- 1 tablespoon paprika
- 1 tablespoon garlic powder
- 1 tablespoon onion powder
- 1 tablespoon freshly ground black pepper
- 1 teaspoon Italian seasoning
- 1 teaspoon salt
- ½ teaspoon ground cumin
- ½ teaspoon cayenne pepper
- 4 tablespoons (½ stick) unsalted butter, melted
- ¼ cup avocado oil
- 4 boneless, skinless chicken breasts (about 2 pounds), halved crosswise

Directions:
1. Insert the Grill Grate and close the hood. Select GRILL, set the temperature to HI, and set the time to 10 minutes. Select START/STOP to begin preheating.
2. In a small bowl, combine the paprika, garlic powder, onion powder, black pepper, Italian seasoning, salt, cumin, and cayenne pepper.
3. In a separate small bowl, whisk together the butter and avocado oil. Lightly coat the chicken breasts on both sides with the butter-and-oil mixture, and then season both sides with the spice mix to get a nice coating.
4. When the unit beeps to signify it has preheated, open the hood and place the seasoned chicken on the Grill Grate. Close the hood and grill for 5 minutes.
5. After 5 minutes, open the hood and flip the chicken. Close the hood and cook for 5 minutes more.
6. When cooking is complete, remove the chicken from the grill and serve.

Turkey Jerky

Servings: 2 | Cooking Time: 3 To 5 Hours

Ingredients:
- 1 pound turkey breast, very thinly sliced
- 1 cup soy sauce
- 2 tablespoons light brown sugar, packed
- 2 tablespoons Worcestershire sauce
- ½ teaspoon garlic powder
- ½ teaspoon onion powder
- ½ teaspoon red pepper flakes

Directions:
1. In a resealable bag, combine the turkey, soy sauce, brown sugar, Worcestershire sauce, garlic powder, onion powder, and red pepper flakes. Massage the turkey slices so all are fully coated in the marinade. Seal the bag and refrigerate overnight.
2. An hour before you plan to put the turkey in the dehydrator, remove the turkey slices from the marinade and place them between two paper towels to dry out and come to room temperature.
3. Once dried, lay the turkey slices flat in the Crisper Basket in a single layer. Insert the Crisper Basket in the Cooking Pot and close the hood. Select DEHYDRATE, set the temperature to 150°F, and set the time to 5 hours. Select START/STOP.
4. After 3 hours, check for desired doneness. Continue dehydrating for up to 2 more hours, if desired.
5. When cooking is complete, the jerky should have a dry texture. Remove from the basket and serve, or store in a resealable bag in the refrigerator for up to 2 weeks.

Glazed Duck With Cherry Sauce

Ingredients:
- 1 whole duck, split in half, back and rib bones removed, fat trimmed
- 1 teaspoon olive oil
- Salt and freshly ground black pepper, to taste
- Cherry Sauce:
- 1 tablespoon butter
- 1 shallot, minced
- ½ cup sherry
- 1 cup chicken stock
- 1 teaspoon white wine vinegar
- ¾ cup cherry preserves
- 1 teaspoon fresh thyme leaves
- Salt and freshly ground black pepper, to taste

Directions:
1. Insert the Crisper Basket and close the hood. Select AIR CRISP, set the temperature to 400ºF, and set the time to 25 minutes. Select START/STOP to begin preheating.
2. On a clean work surface, rub the duck with olive oil, then sprinkle with salt and ground black pepper to season.
3. Place the duck in the basket, breast side up. Close the hood and AIR CRISP for 25 minutes or until well browned. Flip the duck during the last 10 minutes.
4. Meanwhile, make the cherry sauce: Heat the butter in a nonstick skillet over medium-high heat or until melted.
5. Add the shallot and sauté for 5 minutes or until lightly browned.
6. Add the sherry and simmer for 6 minutes or until it reduces in half.
7. Add the chicken stick, white wine vinegar, and cherry preserves. Stir to combine well. Simmer for 6 more minutes or until thickened.
8. Fold in the thyme leaves and sprinkle with salt and ground black pepper. Stir to mix well.
9. When cooking of the duck is complete, glaze the duck with a quarter of the cherry sauce, then AIR CRISP for another 4 minutes.
10. Flip the duck and glaze with another quarter of the cherry sauce. AIR CRISP for an additional 3 minutes.
11. Transfer the duck on a large plate and serve with remaining cherry sauce.

Roasted Cajun Turkey

Ingredients:
- 2 pounds turkey thighs, skinless and boneless
- 1 red onion, sliced
- 2 bell peppers, sliced
- 1 habanero pepper, minced
- 1 carrot, sliced
- 1 tablespoon Cajun seasoning mix
- 1 tablespoon fish sauce
- 2 cups chicken broth
- Nonstick cooking spray

Directions:
1. Select ROAST, set the temperature to 360ºF, and set the time to 30 minutes. Select START/STOP to begin preheating.
2. Spritz the bottom and sides of the pot with nonstick cooking spray.
3. Arrange the turkey thighs in the pot. Add the onion, peppers, and carrot. Sprinkle with Cajun seasoning. Add the fish sauce and chicken broth.
4. Close the hood and ROAST for 30 minutes until cooked through. Serve warm.

Herbed Grilled Chicken Thighs

Servings: 4 | Cooking Time: 13 Minutes

Ingredients:
- Grated zest of 2 lemons
- Juice of 2 lemons
- 3 sprigs fresh rosemary, leaves finely chopped
- 3 sprigs fresh sage, leaves finely chopped
- 2 garlic cloves, minced
- ¼ teaspoon red pepper flakes
- ¼ cup canola oil
- Sea salt
- 4 boneless chicken thighs

Directions:
1. In a small bowl, whisk together the lemon zest and juice, rosemary, sage, garlic, red pepper flakes, and oil. Season with salt.
2. Place the chicken and lemon-herb mixture in a large resealable plastic bag or container. Toss to coat evenly. Refrigerate the chicken for at least 30 minutes.
3. Insert the Grill Grate and close the hood. Select GRILL, set the temperature to HIGH, and set the time to 13 minutes. Select START/STOP to begin preheating.
4. When the unit beeps to signify it has preheated, place the chicken on the Grill Grate. Close the hood and GRILL for 10 to 13 minutes.
5. Cooking is complete when the internal temperature of the chicken reaches at least 165ºF on a food thermometer.

Dill Chicken Strips

Servings: 4 | Cooking Time: 10 Minutes

Ingredients:
- 2 whole boneless, skinless chicken breasts, halved lengthwise
- 1 cup Italian dressing
- 3 cups finely crushed potato chips
- 1 tablespoon dried dill weed
- 1 tablespoon garlic powder
- 1 large egg, beaten
- Cooking spray

Directions:
1. In a large resealable bag, combine the chicken and Italian dressing. Seal the bag and refrigerate to marinate at least 1 hour.
2. In a shallow dish, stir together the potato chips, dill, and garlic powder. Place the beaten egg in a second shallow dish.
3. Remove the chicken from the marinade. Roll the chicken pieces in the egg and the potato chip mixture, coating thoroughly.
4. Select BAKE, set the temperature to 325ºF, and set the time to 10 minutes. Select START/STOP to begin preheating.
5. Place the coated chicken in a baking pan and spritz with cooking spray.
6. Place the pan directly in the pot. Close the hood and BAKE for 5 minutes. Flip the chicken, spritz it with cooking spray, and bake for 5 minutes more until the outsides are crispy and the insides are no longer pink. Serve immediately.

Turkey And Cauliflower Meatloaf

Servings: 6 | Cooking Time: 50 Minutes

Ingredients:
- 2 pounds lean ground turkey
- 1⅓ cups riced cauliflower
- 2 large eggs, lightly beaten
- ¼ cup almond flour
- ⅔ cup chopped yellow or white onion
- 1 teaspoon ground dried turmeric
- 1 teaspoon ground cumin
- 1 teaspoon ground coriander
- 1 tablespoon minced garlic
- 1 teaspoon salt
- 1 teaspoon ground black pepper
- Cooking spray

Directions:
1. Select BAKE, set the temperature to 350ºF, and set the time to 25 minutes. Select START/STOP to begin preheating.
2. Spritz a loaf pan with cooking spray.
3. Combine all the ingredients in a large bowl. Stir to mix well. Pour half of the mixture in the prepared loaf pan and press with a spatula to coat the bottom evenly. Spritz the mixture with cooking spray.
4. Place the pan directly in the pot. Close the hood and BAKE for 25 minutes, or until the meat is well browned and the internal temperature reaches at least 165ºF. Repeat with remaining mixture.
5. Remove the loaf pan from the grill and serve immediately.

Honey Rosemary Chicken

Servings: 4 | Cooking Time: 20 Minutes

Ingredients:
- ¼ cup balsamic vinegar
- ¼ cup honey
- 2 tablespoons olive oil
- 1 tablespoon dried rosemary leaves
- 1 teaspoon salt
- ½ teaspoon freshly ground black pepper
- 2 whole boneless, skinless chicken breasts, halved
- Cooking spray

Directions:
1. In a large resealable bag, combine the vinegar, honey, olive oil, rosemary, salt, and pepper. Add the chicken pieces, seal the bag, and refrigerate to marinate for at least 2 hours.
2. Insert the Crisper Basket and close the hood. Select BAKE, set the temperature to 325ºF, and set the time to 20 minutes. Select START/STOP to begin preheating.
3. Line the Crisper Basket with parchment paper.
4. Remove the chicken from the marinade and place it on the parchment. Spritz with cooking spray.
5. Close the hood and BAKE for 10 minutes. Flip the chicken, spritz it with cooking spray, and bake for 10 minutes more until the internal temperature reaches 165ºF and the chicken is no longer pink inside. Let sit for 5 minutes before serving.

Duck Breasts With Marmalade Balsamic Glaze

Servings: 4 | Cooking Time: 13 Minutes

Ingredients:
- 4 skin-on duck breasts
- 1 teaspoon salt
- ¼ cup orange marmalade
- 1 tablespoon white balsamic vinegar
- ¾ teaspoon ground black pepper

Directions:
1. Insert the Crisper Basket and close the hood. Select AIR CRISP, set the temperature to 400ºF, and set the time to 10 minutes. Select START/STOP to begin preheating.
2. Cut 10 slits into the skin of the duck breasts, then sprinkle with salt on both sides.
3. Place the breasts in the basket, skin side up. Close the hood and AIR CRISP for 10 minutes.
4. Meanwhile, combine the remaining ingredients in a small bowl. Stir to mix well.
5. When the frying is complete, brush the duck skin with the marmalade mixture. Flip the breast and AIR CRISP for 3 more minutes or until the skin is crispy and the breast is well browned.
6. Serve immediately.

SAUCES, DIPS, AND DRESSINGS

SAUCES, DIPS, AND DRESSINGS

Garlic Lime Tahini Dressing

Servings:1 | Cooking Time: 0 Minutes

Ingredients:
- ⅓ cup tahini
- 3 tablespoons filtered water
- 2 tablespoons freshly squeezed lime juice
- 1 tablespoon apple cider vinegar
- 1 teaspoon lime zest
- 1½ teaspoons raw honey
- ¼ teaspoon garlic powder
- ¼ teaspoon salt

Directions:
1. Whisk together the tahini, water, vinegar, lime juice, lime zest, honey, salt, and garlic powder in a small bowl until well emulsified.
2. Serve immediately, or refrigerate in an airtight container for to 1 week.

Ginger Sweet Sauce

Servings:1 | Cooking Time: 5 Minutes

Ingredients:
- 3 tablespoons ketchup
- 2 tablespoons water
- 2 tablespoons maple syrup
- 1 tablespoon rice vinegar
- 2 teaspoons peeled minced fresh ginger root
- 2 teaspoons soy sauce (or tamari, which is a gluten-free option)
- 1 teaspoon cornstarch

Directions:
1. In a small saucepan over medium heat, combine all the ingredients and stir continuously for 5 minutes, or until slightly thickened.
2. Enjoy warm or cold.

Lemon Dijon Vinaigrette

Servings:6 | Cooking Time: 0 Minutes

Ingredients:
- ¼ cup extra-virgin olive oil
- 1 garlic clove, minced
- 2 tablespoons freshly squeezed lemon juice
- 1 teaspoon Dijon mustard
- ½ teaspoon raw honey
- ¼ teaspoon salt
- ¼ teaspoon dried basil

Directions:
1. Place all the ingredients in a mason jar. Cover and shake vigorously until thoroughly mixed and well emulsified.
2. Serve chilled.

Pico De Gallo

Servings: 2 | Cooking Time: 0 Minutes

Ingredients:
- 3 large tomatoes, chopped
- ½ small red onion, diced
- ⅛ cup chopped fresh cilantro
- 3 garlic cloves, chopped
- 2 tablespoons chopped pickled jalapeño pepper
- 1 tablespoon lime juice
- ¼ teaspoon pink Himalayan salt (optional)

Directions:
1. In a medium bowl, combine all the ingredients and mix with a wooden spoon.

Cashew Vodka Sauce

Servings:3 | Cooking Time: 5 Minutes

Ingredients:
- ¾ cup raw cashews
- ¼ cup boiling water
- 1 tablespoon olive oil
- 4 garlic cloves, minced
- 1½ cups unsweetened almond milk
- 1 tablespoon arrowroot powder
- 1 teaspoon salt
- 1 tablespoon nutritional yeast
- 1¼ cups marinara sauce

Directions:
1. Put the cashews in a heatproof bowl and add boiling water to cover. Let soak for 10 minutes. Drain the cashews and place them in a blender. Add ¼ cup boiling water and blend for 1 to 2 minutes or until creamy. Set aside.
2. In a small saucepan, heat the olive oil over medium heat. Add the garlic and sauté for 2 minutes until golden. Whisk in the almond milk, arrowroot powder, and salt. Bring to a simmer. Continue to simmer, whisking frequently, for about 5 minutes or until the sauce thickens.
3. Carefully transfer the hot almond milk mixture to the blender with the cashews. Blend for 30 seconds to combine, then add the nutritional yeast and marinara sauce. Blend for 1 minute or until creamy.

Creamy Ranch Dressing

Servings: 8 | Cooking Time: 0 Minutes

Ingredients:
- 1 cup plain Greek yogurt
- ¼ cup chopped fresh dill
- 2 tablespoons chopped fresh chives
- Zest of 1 lemon
- 1 garlic clove, minced
- ½ teaspoon sea salt
- ⅛ teaspoon freshly cracked black pepper

Directions:
1. Mix together the yogurt, dill, chives, lemon zest, garlic, sea salt, and pepper in a small bowl and whisk to combine.
2. Serve chilled.

Balsamic Dressing

Servings:1 | Cooking Time: 0 Minutes

Ingredients:
- 2 tablespoons Dijon mustard
- ¼ cup balsamic vinegar
- ¾ cup olive oil

Directions:
1. Put all ingredients in a jar with a tight-fitting lid. Put on the lid and shake vigorously until thoroughly combined. Refrigerate until ready to use and shake well before serving.

Hummus

Servings: 2 | Cooking Time: 0 Minutes

Ingredients:
- 1 can chickpeas, drained and rinsed
- ¼ cup tahini
- 3 tablespoons cold water
- 2 tablespoons freshly squeezed lemon juice
- 1 garlic clove
- ½ teaspoon turmeric powder
- ⅛ teaspoon black pepper
- Pinch of pink Himalayan salt

Directions:
1. Combine all the ingredients in a food processor and blend until smooth.

Cashew Pesto

Servings:1 | Cooking Time: 0 Minutes

Ingredients:
- ¼ cup raw cashews
- Juice of 1 lemon
- 2 garlic cloves
- ⅓ red onion
- 1 tablespoon olive oil
- 4 cups basil leaves, packed
- 1 cup wheatgrass
- ¼ cup water
- ¼ teaspoon salt

Directions:
1. Put the cashews in a heatproof bowl and add boiling water to cover. Soak for 5 minutes and then drain.
2. Put all ingredients in a blender and blend for 2 to 3 minutes or until fully combined.

Cashew Ranch Dressing

Servings: 12 | Cooking Time: 0 Minutes

Ingredients:
- 1 cup cashews, soaked in warm water for at least 1 hour
- ½ cup water
- 2 tablespoons freshly squeezed lemon juice
- 1 tablespoon vinegar
- 1 teaspoon garlic powder
- 1 teaspoon onion powder
- 2 teaspoons dried dill

Directions:
1. In a food processor, combine the cashews, water, lemon juice, vinegar, garlic powder, and onion powder. Blend until creamy and smooth. Add the dill and pulse a few times until combined.

DESSERTS

DESSERTS

Orange Cake

Servings: 8 | Cooking Time: 23 Minutes

Ingredients:
- Nonstick baking spray with flour
- 1¼ cups all-purpose flour
- ⅓ cup yellow cornmeal
- ¾ cup white sugar
- 1 teaspoon baking soda
- ¼ cup safflower oil
- 1¼ cups orange juice, divided
- 1 teaspoon vanilla
- ¼ cup powdered sugar

Directions:
1. Select BAKE, set the temperature to 350ºF, and set the time to 23 minutes. Select START/STOP to begin preheating.
2. Spray a baking pan with nonstick spray and set aside.
3. In a medium bowl, combine the flour, cornmeal, sugar, baking soda, safflower oil, 1 cup of the orange juice and vanilla, and mix well.
4. Pour the batter into the baking pan. Place the pan directly in the pot. Close the hood and BAKE for 23 minutes or until a toothpick inserted in the center of the cake comes out clean.
5. Remove the cake from the grill and place on a cooling rack. Using a toothpick, make about 20 holes in the cake.
6. In a small bowl, combine remaining ¼ cup of orange juice and the powdered sugar and stir well. Drizzle this mixture over the hot cake slowly so the cake absorbs it.
7. Cool completely, then cut into wedges to serve.

Mini Brownie Cakes

Servings:4 | Cooking Time: 15 Minutes

Ingredients:
- 8 tablespoons (1 stick) unsalted butter
- 2 large eggs
- ¼ cup unsweetened cocoa powder
- ½ cup granulated sugar
- ½ teaspoon vanilla extract
- ⅛ teaspoon salt
- ½ cup all-purpose flour

Directions:
1. Cut the butter into quarters and divide them between 2 (6-ounce) ramekins. Insert the Cooking Pot, place the ramekins in the pot, and close the hood. Select GRILL, set the temperature to LO, and set the time to 15 minutes. Select START/STOP to begin preheating. After 3 minutes of preheating (set a separate timer), use grill mitts to remove the ramekins and set aside. Close the hood to continue preheating.
2. While the unit is preheating, in a large bowl, whisk the eggs together, then add the cocoa powder, sugar, vanilla, and salt. Sift or gradually shake the flour into the bowl as you continue mixing. Then stir in the melted butter to form a smooth batter. Divide the batter evenly among 4 (6-ounce) ramekins, filling them no more than three-quarters full.
3. When the unit beeps to signify it has preheated, place the ramekins in the Cooking Pot. Close the hood and cook for 15 minutes.
4. When cooking is complete, open the hood and remove the ramekins. The brownies are done when a toothpick inserted in the center comes out clean. (Cooking them for 15 minutes usually gives the brownies a crisp crust with a fudgy center. Add another 3 to 5 minutes if you wish to cook the center all the way through.)

Pound Cake With Mixed Berries

Servings: 6 | Cooking Time: 8 Minutes

Ingredients:

- 3 tablespoons unsalted butter, at room temperature
- 6 slices pound cake, sliced about 1-inch thick
- 1 cup fresh raspberries
- 1 cup fresh blueberries
- 3 tablespoons sugar
- ½ tablespoon fresh mint, minced

Directions:

1. Insert the Grill Grate and close the hood. Select GRILL, set the temperature to MAX, and set the time to 8 minutes. Select START/STOP to begin preheating.
2. While the unit is preheating, evenly spread the butter on both sides of each slice of pound cake.
3. When the unit beeps to signify it has preheated, place the pound cake on the Grill Grate. Close the hood and GRILL for 2 minutes.
4. After 2 minutes, flip the pound cake and GRILL for 2 minutes more, until golden brown. Repeat steps 3 and 4 for all of the pound cake slices.
5. While the pound cake grills, in a medium mixing bowl, combine the raspberries, blueberries, sugar, and mint.
6. When cooking is complete, plate the cake slices and serve topped with the berry mixture.

Curry Peaches, Pears, And Plums

Servings: 6 To 8 | Cooking Time: 5 Minutes

Ingredients:

- 2 peaches
- 2 firm pears
- 2 plums
- 2 tablespoons melted butter
- 1 tablespoon honey
- 2 to 3 teaspoons curry powder

Directions:

1. Insert the Crisper Basket and close the hood. Select BAKE, set the temperature to 325ºF, and set the time to 8 minutes. Select START/STOP to begin preheating.
2. Cut the peaches in half, remove the pits, and cut each half in half again. Cut the pears in half, core them, and remove the stem. Cut each half in half again. Do the same with the plums.
3. Spread a large sheet of heavy-duty foil on the work surface. Arrange the fruit on the foil and drizzle with the butter and honey. Sprinkle with the curry powder.
4. Wrap the fruit in the foil, making sure to leave some air space in the packet.
5. Put the foil package in the basket. Close the hood and BAKE for 5 to 8 minutes, shaking the basket once during the cooking time, until the fruit is soft.
6. Serve immediately.

Chocolate Molten Cake

Servings: 4 | Cooking Time: 10 Minutes

Ingredients:

- 3.5 ounces butter, melted
- 3½ tablespoons sugar
- 3.5 ounces chocolate, melted
- 1½ tablespoons flour
- 2 eggs

Directions:

1. Select BAKE, set the temperature to 375ºF, and set the time to 10 minutes. Select START/STOP to begin preheating.
2. Grease four ramekins with a little butter.
3. Rigorously combine the eggs, butter, and sugar before stirring in the melted chocolate.
4. Slowly fold in the flour.
5. Spoon an equal amount of the mixture into each ramekin.
6. Put them in the pot. Close the hood and BAKE for 10 minutes.
7. Put the ramekins upside-down on plates and let the cakes fall out. Serve hot.

Grilled Apple Fries With Caramel Cream Cheese Dip

Servings: 4 | Cooking Time: 5 Minutes

Ingredients:
- 4 apples, such as Honeycrisp, Gala, Pink Lady, or Granny Smith, peeled, cored, and sliced
- ¼ cup heavy (whipping) cream
- 1 tablespoon granulated sugar
- ¼ teaspoon cinnamon
- ¼ cup all-purpose flour
- 4 ounces cream cheese, at room temperature
- 1 tablespoon caramel sauce
- 1 tablespoon light brown sugar, packed

Directions:
1. Insert the Grill Grate and close the hood. Select GRILL, set the temperature to MAX, and set the time to 5 minutes. Select START/STOP to begin preheating.
2. In a large bowl, toss the apple slices with the heavy cream, granulated sugar, and cinnamon to coat. Slowly shake in the flour and continue mixing to coat.
3. In a small bowl, mix together the cream cheese, caramel sauce, and brown sugar until smooth. Set aside.
4. When the unit beeps to signify it has preheated, place the apples on the Grill Grate in a single layer. Close the hood and grill for 2 minutes, 30 seconds.
5. After 2 minutes, 30 seconds, open the hood and flip and toss the apples around. Close the hood and cook for 2 minutes, 30 seconds more.
6. When cooking is complete, open the hood and remove the apple chips from the grill. Serve with the sauce.

Chocolate And Peanut Butter Lava Cupcakes

Servings: 8 | Cooking Time: 10 To 13 Minutes

Ingredients:
- Nonstick baking spray with flour
- 1⅓ cups chocolate cake mix
- 1 egg
- 1 egg yolk
- ¼ cup safflower oil
- ¼ cup hot water
- ⅓ cup sour cream
- 3 tablespoons peanut butter
- 1 tablespoon powdered sugar

Directions:
1. Select BAKE, set the temperature to 350ºF, and set the time to 13 minutes. Select START/STOP to begin preheating.
2. Double up 16 foil muffin cups to make 8 cups. Spray each lightly with nonstick spray; set aside.
3. In a medium bowl, combine the cake mix, egg, egg yolk, safflower oil, water, and sour cream, and beat until combined.
4. In a small bowl, combine the peanut butter and powdered sugar and mix well. Form this mixture into 8 balls.
5. Spoon about ¼ cup of the chocolate batter into each muffin cup and top with a peanut butter ball. Spoon remaining batter on top of the peanut butter balls to cover them.
6. Arrange the cups in the pot, leaving some space between each. Place the pan directly in the pot. Close the hood and BAKE for 10 to 13 minutes or until the tops look dry and set.
7. Let the cupcakes cool for about 10 minutes, then serve warm.

Grilled Strawberry Pound Cake

Servings: 8 | Cooking Time: 8 Minutes

Ingredients:

- 1 loaf pound cake, cut into ¼-inch-thick slices (8 slices)
- 4 tablespoons (½ stick) unsalted butter, melted
- 2 cups strawberries, sliced
- 1 tablespoon granulated sugar
- Juice of ¼ lemon

Directions:

1. Insert the Grill Grate and close the hood. Select GRILL, set the temperature to HI, and set the time to 8 minutes. Select START/STOP to begin preheating.
2. While the unit is preheating, brush both sides of the pound cake slices with the melted butter. In a small bowl, combine the strawberries, sugar, and lemon juice.
3. When the unit beeps to signify it has preheated, place 4 slices of pound cake on the Grill Grate. Close the hood and grill for 2 minutes.
4. After 2 minutes, open the hood and flip the pound cake slices. Top each with ¼ cup of strawberries. Close the hood and cook for 2 minutes.
5. After 2 minutes, open the hood and carefully remove the grilled pound cake. Repeat steps 3 and 4 with the remaining pound cake and strawberries. Serve.

Sweet Potato Donuts

Servings:12 | Cooking Time: 52 Minutes

Ingredients:

- 3 cups water
- 1 medium white sweet potato
- ⅔ cup all-purpose flour, plus more for dusting
- ½ cup granulated sugar
- Avocado oil

Directions:

1. Insert the Cooking Pot, pour in the water, and close the hood. Select BROIL, set the temperature to 500°F, and set the time to 20 minutes. Select START/STOP to begin preheating.
2. While the unit is preheating, peel the sweet potato and cut it into chunks.
3. When the unit beeps to signify it has preheated, add the sweet potato to the Cooking Pot, making sure the chunks are fully submerged in the water. Close the hood and cook for 20 minutes.
4. After 20 minutes, open the hood and pierce a potato chunk to check for doneness—it should be easy to slice into. Remove and drain the sweet potatoes.
5. In a large bowl, mash the sweet potato with a masher or fork. When it has cooled down, add ⅔ cup of flour and the sugar and mix until well combined. The dough will be sticky. Dust a clean work surface with some flour. Roll and knead the dough until it is no longer sticky and holds its form, using more flour as needed.
6. Divide the dough in half and then cut each half into 6 equal-size pieces. Roll each piece of dough into a cylinder about 4 inches long.
7. Insert the Cooking Pot and close the hood. Select GRILL, set the temperature to HI, and set the time to 16 minutes. Select START/STOP to begin preheating.
8. While the unit is preheating, brush avocado oil on a 6-ring donut pan and place 6 donuts in the molds. Brush more avocado oil on top.
9. When the unit beeps to signify it has preheated, place the donut pan in the Cooking Pot. Close the hood and grill for 8 minutes.
10. When cooking is complete, remove the pan and transfer the donuts to a rack to cool.
11. Repeat steps 8 through 10 with the remaining donuts. Serve.

Apple, Peach, And Cranberry Crisp

Servings: 8 | Cooking Time: 12 Minutes

Ingredients:
- 1 apple, peeled and chopped
- 2 peaches, peeled and chopped
- $\frac{1}{3}$ cup dried cranberries
- 2 tablespoons honey
- $\frac{1}{3}$ cup brown sugar
- ¼ cup flour
- ½ cup oatmeal
- 3 tablespoons softened butter

Directions:
1. Select BAKE, set the temperature to 370ºF, and set the time to 12 minutes. Select START/STOP to begin preheating.
2. In a baking pan, combine the apple, peaches, cranberries, and honey, and mix well.
3. In a medium bowl, combine the brown sugar, flour, oatmeal, and butter, and mix until crumbly. Sprinkle this mixture over the fruit in the pan.
4. Place the pan directly in the pot. Close the hood and BAKE for 10 to 12 minutes or until the fruit is bubbly and the topping is golden brown. Serve warm.

Black And White Brownies

Servings:1 | Cooking Time: 20 Minutes

Ingredients:
- 1 egg
- ¼ cup brown sugar
- 2 tablespoons white sugar
- 2 tablespoons safflower oil
- 1 teaspoon vanilla
- $\frac{1}{3}$ cup all-purpose flour
- ¼ cup cocoa powder
- ¼ cup white chocolate chips
- Nonstick cooking spray

Directions:
1. Select BAKE, set the temperature to 340ºF, and set the time to 20 minutes. Select START/STOP to begin preheating.
2. Spritz a baking pan with nonstick cooking spray.
3. Whisk together the egg, brown sugar, and white sugar in a medium bowl. Mix in the safflower oil and vanilla and stir to combine.
4. Add the flour and cocoa powder and stir just until incorporated. Fold in the white chocolate chips.
5. Scrape the batter into the prepared baking pan.
6. Place the pan directly in the pot. Close the hood and BAKE for 20 minutes, or until the brownie springs back when touched lightly with your fingers.
7. Transfer to a wire rack and let cool for 30 minutes before slicing to serve.

Cinnamon Candied Apples

Servings: 4 | Cooking Time: 12 Minutes

Ingredients:
- 1 cup packed light brown sugar
- 2 teaspoons ground cinnamon
- 2 medium Granny Smith apples, peeled and diced

Directions:
1. Select BAKE, set the temperature to 350ºF, and set the time to 12 minutes. Select START/STOP to begin preheating.
2. Thoroughly combine the brown sugar and cinnamon in a medium bowl.
3. Add the apples to the bowl and stir until well coated. Transfer the apples to a baking pan.
4. Place the pan directly in the pot. Close the hood and BAKE for 9 minutes. Stir the apples once and bake for an additional 3 minutes until softened.
5. Serve warm.

Cinnamon-sugar Dessert Chips

Servings: 4 | Cooking Time: 10 Minutes

Ingredients:
- 10 (6-inch) flour tortillas
- 8 tablespoons (1 stick) unsalted butter, melted
- 1 tablespoon cinnamon
- ¼ cup granulated sugar
- ½ cup chocolate syrup, for dipping

Directions:
1. Insert the Grill Grate and close the hood. Select GRILL, set the temperature to HI, and set the time to 10 minutes. Select START/STOP to begin preheating.
2. While the unit is preheating, cut the tortillas into 6 equal wedges. In a large resealable bag, combine the tortillas, butter, cinnamon, and sugar and shake vigorously to coat the tortillas.
3. When the unit beeps to signify it has preheated, add half the tortillas to the Grill Grate. Close the hood and cook for 2 minutes, 30 seconds.
4. After 2 minutes, 30 seconds, open the hood and use a spatula to quickly flip the chips or move them around. Close the hood and cook for 2 minutes, 30 seconds more.
5. After 2 minutes, 30 seconds, open the hood and remove the grilled chips and repeat the process with the remaining tortillas.
6. Serve with the chocolate syrup for dipping.

Vanilla Scones

Servings:18 | Cooking Time: 15 Minutes

Ingredients:
- For the scones
- 2 cups almond flour
- ¼ cup granulated sugar
- ¼ teaspoon salt
- 1 tablespoon baking powder
- 2 large eggs
- 1 teaspoon vanilla extract
- 4 tablespoons (½ stick) unsalted butter, melted
- 2 tablespoons heavy (whipping) cream
- For the icing
- 1 cup powdered sugar
- 2 tablespoons heavy (whipping) cream
- 1 tablespoon vanilla extract

Directions:
1. In a large bowl, combine the almond flour, granulated sugar, salt, and baking powder. In another large bowl, whisk the eggs, then whisk in the vanilla, butter, and heavy cream. Add the dry ingredients to the wet and mix just until a dough forms.
2. Insert the Cooking Pot and close the hood. Select BAKE, set the temperature to 325°F, and set the time to 15 minutes. Select START/STOP to begin preheating.
3. While the unit is preheating, divide the dough into 3 equal pieces. Shape each piece into a disc about 1 inch thick and 5 inches in diameter. Cut each into 6 wedges, like slicing a pizza.
4. When the unit beeps to signify it has preheated, place the scones in the Cooking Pot, spacing them apart so they don't bake together. Close the hood and cook for 15 minutes.
5. While the scones are baking, in a small bowl, combine the powdered sugar, heavy cream, and vanilla. Stir until smooth.
6. After 15 minutes, open the hood and remove the scones. They are done baking when they have turned a light golden brown. Place on a wire rack to cool to room temperature. Drizzle the icing over the scones, or pour a tablespoonful on the top of each scone for an even glaze.

Grilled Banana S'mores

Ingredients:
- 4 large bananas
- 1 cup milk chocolate chips
- 1 cup mini marshmallows
- 4 graham crackers, crushed

Directions:
1. Insert the Cooking Pot and close the hood. Select GRILL, set the temperature to HI, and set the time to 6 minutes. Select START/STOP to begin preheating.
2. While the unit is preheating, prepare the banana boats. Starting at the bottom of a banana, slice the peel lengthwise up one side and then the opposite side. Pull the top half of the peel back, revealing the fruit underneath, but keeping the bottom of the banana peel intact. With a spoon, carefully scoop out some of the banana. (Eat it or set it aside.) Repeat with each banana. Equally divide the chocolate chips and marshmallows between the banana boats.
3. When the unit beeps to signify it has preheated, place the bananas in the Cooking Pot. Close the hood and cook for 6 minutes.
4. When cooking is complete, remove the bananas from the grill and sprinkle the crushed graham crackers on top. Serve.

Orange Coconut Cake

Servings: 6 | Cooking Time: 17 Minutes

Ingredients:
- 1 stick butter, melted
- ¾ cup granulated Swerve
- 2 eggs, beaten
- ¾ cup coconut flour
- ¼ teaspoon salt
- $\frac{1}{3}$ teaspoon grated nutmeg
- $\frac{1}{3}$ cup coconut milk
- 1¼ cups almond flour
- ½ teaspoon baking powder
- 2 tablespoons unsweetened orange jam
- Cooking spray

Directions:
1. Select BAKE, set the temperature to 355ºF, and set the time to 17 minutes. Select START/STOP to begin preheating.
2. Coat a baking pan with cooking spray. Set aside.
3. In a large mixing bowl, whisk together the melted butter and granulated Swerve until fluffy.
4. Mix in the beaten eggs and whisk again until smooth. Stir in the coconut flour, salt, and nutmeg and gradually pour in the coconut milk. Add the remaining ingredients and stir until well incorporated.
5. Scrape the batter into the baking pan.
6. Place the pan directly in the pot. Close the hood and BAKE for 17 minutes until the top of the cake springs back when gently pressed with your fingers.
7. Remove from the grill to a wire rack to cool. Serve chilled.

Peanut Butter-chocolate Bread Pudding

Servings: 8 | Cooking Time: 10 To 12 Minutes

Ingredients:
- 1 egg
- 1 egg yolk
- ¾ cup chocolate milk
- 3 tablespoons brown sugar
- 3 tablespoons peanut butter
- 2 tablespoons cocoa powder
- 1 teaspoon vanilla
- 5 slices firm white bread, cubed
- Nonstick cooking spray

Directions:
1. Select BAKE, set the temperature to 330ºF, and set the time to 12 minutes. Select START/STOP to begin preheating.
2. Spritz a baking pan with nonstick cooking spray.
3. Whisk together the egg, egg yolk, chocolate milk, brown sugar, peanut butter, cocoa powder, and vanilla until well combined.
4. Fold in the bread cubes and stir to mix well. Allow the bread soak for 10 minutes.
5. When ready, transfer the egg mixture to the prepared baking pan.
6. Place the pan directly in the pot. Close the hood and BAKE for 10 to 12 minutes, or until the pudding is just firm to the touch.
7. Serve at room temperature.

Orange And Anise Cake

Servings: 6 | Cooking Time: 20 Minutes

Ingredients:
- 1 stick butter, at room temperature
- 5 tablespoons liquid monk fruit
- 2 eggs plus 1 egg yolk, beaten
- ⅓ cup hazelnuts, roughly chopped
- 3 tablespoons sugar-free orange marmalade
- 6 ounces unbleached almond flour
- 1 teaspoon baking soda
- ½ teaspoon baking powder
- ½ teaspoon ground cinnamon
- ½ teaspoon ground allspice
- ½ ground anise seed
- Cooking spray

Directions:
1. Select BAKE, set the temperature to 310ºF, and set the time to 20 minutes. Select START/STOP to begin preheating.
2. Lightly spritz a baking pan with cooking spray.
3. In a mixing bowl, whisk the butter and liquid monk fruit until the mixture is pale and smooth. Mix in the beaten eggs, hazelnuts, and marmalade and whisk again until well incorporated.
4. Add the almond flour, baking soda, baking powder, cinnamon, allspice, anise seed and stir to mix well.
5. Scrape the batter into the prepared baking pan. Place the pan directly in the pot. Close the hood and BAKE for 20 minutes, or until the top of the cake springs back when gently pressed with your fingers.
6. Transfer to a wire rack and let the cake cool to room temperature. Serve immediately.

Ultimate Skillet Brownies

Servings: 6 | Cooking Time: 40 Minutes

Ingredients:
- ½ cup all-purpose flour
- ¼ cup unsweetened cocoa powder
- ¾ teaspoon sea salt
- 2 large eggs
- 1 tablespoon water
- ½ cup granulated sugar
- ½ cup dark brown sugar
- 1 tablespoon vanilla extract
- 8 ounces semisweet chocolate chips, melted
- ¾ cup unsalted butter, melted
- Nonstick cooking spray

Directions:
1. In a medium bowl, whisk together the flour, cocoa powder, and salt.
2. In a large bowl, whisk together the eggs, water, sugar, brown sugar, and vanilla until smooth.
3. In a microwave-safe bowl, melt the chocolate in the microwave. In a separate microwave-safe bowl, melt the butter.
4. In a separate medium bowl, stir together the chocolate and butter until evenly combined. Whisk into the egg mixture. Then slowly add the dry ingredients, stirring just until incorporated.
5. Remove the Grill Grate from the unit. Select BAKE, set the temperature to 350ºF, and set the time to 40 minutes. Select START/STOP to begin preheating.
6. Meanwhile, lightly grease the baking pan with cooking spray. Pour the batter into the pan, spreading evenly.
7. When the unit beeps to signify it has preheated, place the pan directly in the pot. Close the hood and BAKE for 40 minutes.
8. After 40 minutes, check that baking is complete. A wooden toothpick inserted into the center of the brownies should come out clean.

Fresh Blueberry Cobbler

Servings: 6 | Cooking Time: 30 Minutes

Ingredients:
- 4 cups fresh blueberries
- 1 teaspoon grated lemon zest
- 1 cup sugar, plus 2 tablespoons
- 1 cup all-purpose flour, plus 2 tablespoons
- Juice of 1 lemon
- 2 teaspoons baking powder
- ¼ teaspoon salt
- 6 tablespoons unsalted butter
- ¾ cup whole milk
- ⅛ teaspoon ground cinnamon

Directions:
1. In a medium bowl, combine the blueberries, lemon zest, 2 tablespoons of sugar, 2 tablespoons of flour, and lemon juice.
2. In a medium bowl, combine the remaining 1 cup of flour and 1 cup of sugar, baking powder, and salt. Cut the butter into the flour mixture until it forms an even crumb texture. Stir in the milk until a dough forms.
3. Select BAKE, set the temperature to 350ºF, and set the time to 30 minutes. Select START/STOP to begin preheating.
4. Meanwhile, pour the blueberry mixture into the baking pan, spreading it evenly across the pan. Gently pour the batter over the blueberry mixture, then sprinkle the cinnamon over the top.
5. When the unit beeps to signify it has preheated, place the pan directly in the pot. Close the hood and BAKE for 30 minutes, until lightly golden.
6. When cooking is complete, serve warm.

Chocolate And Coconut Cake

Servings: 6 | Cooking Time: 15 Minutes

Ingredients:
- ½ cup unsweetened chocolate, chopped
- ½ stick butter, at room temperature
- 1 tablespoon liquid stevia
- 1½ cups coconut flour
- 2 eggs, whisked
- ½ teaspoon vanilla extract
- A pinch of fine sea salt
- Cooking spray

Directions:
1. Place the chocolate, butter, and stevia in a microwave-safe bowl. Microwave for about 30 seconds until melted.
2. Let the chocolate mixture cool for 5 to 10 minutes.
3. Add the remaining ingredients to the bowl of chocolate mixture and whisk to incorporate.
4. Select BAKE, set the temperature to 330ºF, and set the time to 15 minutes. Select START/STOP to begin preheating.
5. Lightly spray a baking pan with cooking spray.
6. Scrape the chocolate mixture into the prepared baking pan.
7. Place the pan directly in the pot. Close the hood and BAKE for 15 minutes, or until the top springs back lightly when gently pressed with your fingers.
8. Let the cake cool for 5 minutes and serve.

Rich Chocolate Cookie

Servings: 4 | Cooking Time: 9 Minutes

Ingredients:
- Nonstick baking spray with flour
- 3 tablespoons softened butter
- ⅓ cup plus 1 tablespoon brown sugar
- 1 egg yolk
- ½ cup flour
- 2 tablespoons ground white chocolate
- ¼ teaspoon baking soda
- ½ teaspoon vanilla
- ¾ cup chocolate chips

Directions:
1. Select BAKE, set the temperature to 350ºF, and set the time to 9 minutes. Select START/STOP to begin preheating.
2. In a medium bowl, beat the butter and brown sugar together until fluffy. Stir in the egg yolk.
3. Add the flour, white chocolate, baking soda, and vanilla, and mix well. Stir in the chocolate chips.
4. Line a baking pan with parchment paper. Spray the parchment paper with nonstick baking spray with flour.
5. Spread the batter into the prepared pan, leaving a ½-inch border on all sides.
6. Place the pan directly in the pot. Close the hood and BAKE for 9 minutes or until the cookie is light brown and just barely set.
7. Remove the pan from the grill and let cool for 10 minutes. Remove the cookie from the pan, remove the parchment paper, and let cool on a wire rack.
8. Serve immediately.

Black Forest Pies

Ingredients:
- 3 tablespoons milk or dark chocolate chips
- 2 tablespoons thick, hot fudge sauce
- 2 tablespoons chopped dried cherries
- 1 sheet frozen puff pastry, thawed
- 1 egg white, beaten
- 2 tablespoons sugar
- ½ teaspoon cinnamon

Directions:
1. Insert the Crisper Basket and close the hood. Select BAKE, set the temperature to 350°F, and set the time to 15 minutes. Select START/STOP to begin preheating.
2. In a small bowl, combine the chocolate chips, fudge sauce, and dried cherries.
3. Roll out the puff pastry on a floured surface. Cut into 6 squares with a sharp knife.
4. Divide the chocolate chip mixture into the center of each puff pastry square. Fold the squares in half to make triangles. Firmly press the edges with the tines of a fork to seal.
5. Brush the triangles on all sides sparingly with the beaten egg white. Sprinkle the tops with sugar and cinnamon.
6. Put in the Crisper Basket. Close the hood and BAKE for 15 minutes or until the triangles are golden brown. The filling will be hot, so cool for at least 20 minutes before serving.

Date: _____

MY SHOPPING LIST

Recipe for:

Ingredients:

Equipment:

Description:

Instructions:

Appendix A : Measurement Conversions

BASIC KITCHEN CONVERSIONS & EQUIVALENTS

DRY MEASUREMENTS CONVERSION CHART

3 TEASPOONS = 1 TABLESPOON = 1/16 CUP

6 TEASPOONS = 2 TABLESPOONS = 1/8 CUP

12 TEASPOONS = 4 TABLESPOONS = 1/4 CUP

24 TEASPOONS = 8 TABLESPOONS = 1/2 CUP

36 TEASPOONS = 12 TABLESPOONS = 3/4 CUP

48 TEASPOONS = 16 TABLESPOONS = 1 CUP

METRIC TO US COOKING CONVERSIONS

OVEN TEMPERATURES

120 °C = 250 °F

160 °C = 320 °F

180° C = 350 °F

205 °C = 400 °F

220 °C = 425 °F

LIQUID MEASUREMENTS CONVERSION CHART

8 FLUID OUNCES = 1 CUP = 1/2 PINT = 1/4 QUART

16 FLUID OUNCES = 2 CUPS = 1 PINT = 1/2 QUART

32 FLUID OUNCES = 4 CUPS = 2 PINTS = 1 QUART

 = 1/4 GALLON

128 FLUID OUNCES = 16 CUPS = 8 PINTS = 4 QUARTS = 1 GALLON

BAKING IN GRAMS

1 CUP FLOUR = 140 GRAMS

1 CUP SUGAR = 150 GRAMS

1 CUP POWDERED SUGAR = 160 GRAMS

1 CUP HEAVY CREAM = 235 GRAMS

VOLUME

1 MILLILITER = 1/5 TEASPOON

5 ML = 1 TEASPOON

15 ML = 1 TABLESPOON

240 ML = 1 CUP OR 8 FLUID OUNCES

1 LITER = 34 FL. OUNCES

WEIGHT

1 GRAM = .035 OUNCES

100 GRAMS = 3.5 OUNCES

500 GRAMS = 1.1 POUNDS

1 KILOGRAM = 35 OUNCES

US TO METRIC COOKING CONVERSIONS

1/5 TSP = 1 ML

1 TSP = 5 ML

1 TBSP = 15 ML

1 FL OUNCE = 30 ML

1 CUP = 237 ML

1 PINT (2 CUPS) = 473 ML

1 QUART (4 CUPS) = .95 LITER

1 GALLON (16 CUPS) = 3.8 LITERS

1 OZ = 28 GRAMS

1 POUND = 454 GRAMS

BUTTER

1 CUP BUTTER = 2 STICKS = 8 OUNCES = 230 GRAMS = 8 TABLESPOONS

WHAT DOES 1 CUP EQUAL

1 CUP = 8 FLUID OUNCES

1 CUP = 16 TABLESPOONS

1 CUP = 48 TEASPOONS

1 CUP = 1/2 PINT

1 CUP = 1/4 QUART

1 CUP = 1/16 GALLON

1 CUP = 240 ML

BAKING PAN CONVERSIONS

1 CUP ALL-PURPOSE FLOUR = 4.5 OZ

1 CUP ROLLED OATS = 3 OZ 1 LARGE EGG = 1.7 OZ

1 CUP BUTTER = 8 OZ 1 CUP MILK = 8 OZ

1 CUP HEAVY CREAM = 8.4 OZ

1 CUP GRANULATED SUGAR = 7.1 OZ

1 CUP PACKED BROWN SUGAR = 7.75 OZ

1 CUP VEGETABLE OIL = 7.7 OZ

1 CUP UNSIFTED POWDERED SUGAR = 4.4 OZ

BAKING PAN CONVERSIONS

9-INCH ROUND CAKE PAN = 12 CUPS

10-INCH TUBE PAN =16 CUPS

11-INCH BUNDT PAN = 12 CUPS

9-INCH SPRINGFORM PAN = 10 CUPS

9 X 5 INCH LOAF PAN = 8 CUPS

9-INCH SQUARE PAN = 8 CUPS

Appendix B : Recipes Index

G

H

K

L

Made in the USA
Las Vegas, NV
22 September 2024

95638364R00059